Creative
STAMPING
for Scrapbookers

Step-by-step projects and techniques for stamped pages

MEMORY MAKERS BOOKS

Senior Editor Lydia Rueger

Art Director Nick Nyffeler

Graphic Designers Robin Rozum, Andrea Zocchi

Art Acquisitions Editor Janetta Abucejo Wieneke

Craft Editor Jodi Amidei

Photographer Ken Trujillo

Contributing Photographers Lizzy Creazzo, Brenda Martinez, Jennifer Reeves

Contributing Writers Elizabeth Shaffer Harlan, Heather Marie Wells, Anne Wilbur

Editorial Support Karen Cain, Emily Curry Hitchingham, MaryJo Regier, Dena Twinem

Contributing Memory Makers Masters Susan Cyrus, Jeniece Higgins, Julie Johnson, Andrea Lyn Vetten-Marley, Torrey Miller, Heidi Schueller, Shannon Taylor, Denise Tucker, Samantha Walker, Holle Wiktorek

Hand Model Ann Kitayama

Memory Makers® *Creative Stamping for Scrapbookers*

Published by Memory Makers Books, an imprint of F+W Publications, Inc.

12365 Huron Street, Suite 500, Denver, CO 80234

Phone (800) 254-9124

First edition. Printed in the United States.

09 08 07 06 05 5 4 3 2 1

Library of Congress Cataloging-in-Publication Data

Creative stamping for scrapbookers : step-by-step projects and techniques for stamped pages.
    p. cm.
    Includes bibliographical references and index.
    ISBN 1-892127-54-7
    1. Photograph albums. 2. Photographs--Conservation and restoration. 3. Scrapbooks. 4. Rubber stamp printing. I. Title: Stamping for Scrapbookers. II Memory Makers Books.

TR465.C76 2005
761--dc22

2004063158

Distributed to trade and art markets by

F+W Publications, Inc.

4700 East Galbraith Road, Cincinnati, OH 45236

Phone (800) 289-0963

ISBN 1-892127-54-7

Memory Makers Books is the home of *Memory Makers*, the scrapbook magazine dedicated to educating and inspiring scrapbookers. ATo subscribe, or for more information, call (800) 366-6465. Visit us on the Internet at www.memorymakersmagazine.com.

This book belongs to

_____

Dedicated to rubber stampers who have now become scrapbookers, too. Your love of the art form has kept it alive throughout the years, allowing it to make its way onto scrapbook pages in many forms.

Table of Contents

1 Accents and Embellishments 12

2 Backgrounds 36

Animals
are
such agreeable
friends;
they
ask no questions
they pass
no criticism.

- George Eliot

It's hard to believe that this regal and royal cat got its beginning in a barn, but that's where this story starts. She was born at a farm of our neighbors, Beth and Ernie. Her mother wouldn't come near people and was very skittish. But every time Ernie would go work on the farm, this silly kitten wouldn't leave him alone. She was always following him around and couldn't get enough of human contact. So, one day Beth came knocking on our door, an adorable kitten in her arms. That's all it took. Haley got one look at her and she was instantly part of the family. She was raised with Haley and to this day, she will allow Haley to do things to her that she won't put up with from anyone else. When Haley has a hold of her, she is the most tolerant cat around. But for anyone else.... please, royalty doesn't have to put up with the likes of us.

MEOW

Introduction

Before many faithful *Memory Makers* contributors spent a great deal of their free time working on photo organization, journaling and creative title treatments for scrapbook pages, they were stampers. As some of these stampers have told me over the years, adding scrapbooking to their list of craft skills was an natural transition—many of the stamping techniques they'd refined for card-making work great when paired with photos and journaling.

On the flip side, scrapbookers looking for new challenges often turn to stamping. They've tried every sticker, punch and creative paper technique out there and are seeking to expand their skill set even more. (Our own craft editor and creator of the page shown left, Jodi Amidei, is one of these scrapbookers-turned-stampers.) A few dozen ink pads, stamps and embossing powders later, they've found the creative outlet they were looking for.

Stamping is as addictive as scrapbooking itself because it allows anyone to be an artist. Just by choosing a specific premade image carved into rubber, acrylic or foam, you can achieve the look of detailed hand drawings, soft paintbrush strokes or bold, blocky designs simply by pressing the image to paper. The results are instant, and depending on the different colorants, embossing powders and techniques applied to each stamped image, you'll never end up with the same image twice.

Delve into *Creative Stamping for Scrapbookers* and you'll find a world of step-by-step techniques, innovative page ideas and tips to help you get stamping in your scrapbooks, whether you were a creative stamper or a scrapbooker first.

Lydia

Lydia Rueger, Senior Editor

Basic Stamping Supplies

Walk into any stamping store and you'll see rubber and foam designs by the hundreds, towering stacks of colored ink pads with names like Platinum Planet and Perfect Plumeria, rows of tiny vials filled with shimmering powders and a wide array of other colorants and tools. It's a beautiful sight for avid stampers, but for beginners, it can be difficult to know what to purchase. The following information will help novice stampers determine which products they should invest in dye from the start.

STAMPS

Both rubber and foam stamps are available in a variety of designs. Foam stamps are less expensive but not as durable and don't have a lot of fine detail. Rubber stamps offer greater selection, higher quality and a lifetime of use when well cared for.

Most stamps available in retail stores are mounted stamps, which means that the rubber design is permanently attached to a wood or acrylic handle, called the mount. Mounted stamps are the easiest for beginners, but you can save money by purchasing unmounted stamps—just the rubber design with no cushion or mount. Unmounted-stamp users then purchase a set of acrylic handles in various sizes and temporarily mount each image to the handle as needed. Unmounted stamps also save storage space, but require a commitment to careful organization so that the images are accessible when needed.

INKS

Start with basic black for your first ink pad, and then add a few of your favorite colors. Consider purchasing re-inker—a small bottle of ink that you can use to re-moisten your pad when it begins to dry out. Most inks fall into two categories—dye or pigment. Dye inks dry very quickly and have a thin, transparent effect much like watercolor paint. They are not typically fade-resistant or waterproof, although some companies now manufacture varieties for scrapbooking that are.

Pigment inks, which offer opaque, vibrant color, are a good choice for scrapbook stamping because they are waterproof and fade-resistant. Be aware that pigment inks tend to dry more slowly. Allow 24 hours for complete drying time or set with a heat gun to expedite the process.

Other popular types of inks to consider are:

- Watermark ink: clear pigment ink that turns paper a darker shade than its original color.

- Embossing ink: clear or lightly tinted pigment ink that is specially formulated to hold embossing powder well.

- Solvent ink: ink that is formulated for use on non-porous surfaces such as metal, glass and plastic.

- Chalk ink: a type of dye ink that dries to a matte finish and has the appearance of colored chalk.

- Metallic ink: ink that is available in a variety of colors and has a shimmering finish.

EMBOSSING POWDERS, HEAT GUN AND SPECIAL TRAYS

Embossing powder is basically powdered plastic that looks like very fine glitter. It comes in a large assortment of colors and sizes ranging from ultra fine to coarse. When heated, embossing powder makes a stamped image raised, smooth and shiny. It also sets the ink so that it will not smear or rub off on another page element. The finer the embossing powder, the more detail on the embossed image. Start with a fine or ultra fine embossing powder in black, clear, gold, copper or silver. Extra thick embossing powder has a different purpose than regular embossing powder. When melted, its larger flakes form a thick, pastelike substance, allowing you to stamp impressions into it. When cool, extra thick embossing powder forms a hard enamel-like surface.

For embossing, you'll also need a heat gun—a small hair-dryerlike tool used to melt embossing powder or speed up the drying time of inks. If you think you can substitute a hairdryer for a heat gun, however, think again. Heat guns reach much higher temperatures than hairdryers which is necessary for melting embossing powder.

To contain the mess of embossing powder, purchase a special tray with deep sides designed for stamping projects. The tray catches loose powder and allows you to pour the excess back into its original container through a small spout.

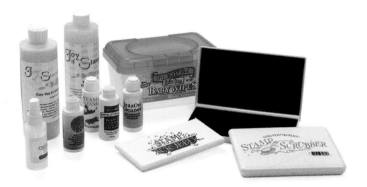

STAMP CLEANERS

Stamps should be cleaned immediately after each use, and there are a variety of solutions specially formulated for stamp cleaning. Simply apply the cleaner to a paper towel or rag and wipe away the excess ink. Most types of ink also can be removed with alcohol-free baby wipes. An old toothbrush is helpful for removing ink from tiny crevices, or you can purchase stamp scrubbing pads made for that purpose.

FUN EXTRAS

While the following products aren't essential for beginner stampers, they can add a little something extra to your projects when you're ready to try something new.

- Brayers: Available in many sizes, brayers are used to create smoothly blended multicolored backgrounds. Apply one ink color at a time to a brayer, then roll across paper. Repeat with other colors for unique backgrounds or photo mats. They are also used to apply ink to large background stamps.

- Roller stamps: Available in a variety of patterns, roller stamps are fun to use for page borders and frames. Snap your pattern of choice into the handle, then roll the design on paper.

- Melting pot: Sprinkle embossing powder in the metal tray and heat to desired temperature to melt the powder. Once melted, you can pour the substance over certain embellishments for a thicker coating, pour it directly into shape molds or dip embellishments.

- Molding mats and molded stylus: When the foam tip of a molded stylus is heated with a light bulb, it becomes soft, allowing you to press a pattern into it using thin sheets of patterned rubber known as molding mats. Reheating the foam allows you to change the image over and over again.

- Finger daubers: These small applicators with a sponge tip fit over your fingertips, allowing more precision and control when applying different colorants to stamped outlines.

Selecting Colorants

A big part of the fun in stamping is deciding how to color your images. These examples will help you see the differences—and often the similarities—between types of colorants. Note how you can achieve a similar look with chalk, metallic rub-ons and chalk stamping ink. If you are on a budget or have limited space to store supplies, purchase only the ones in which the final outcome is different enough to achieve the look you want.

COLORED STAMPING INKS
(Fluid Chalk inks by Clearsnap)

MARKERS
(Marvy Uchida)

COLORED PENCILS
(Sanford)

WATERCOLOR PAINT
(Angora by Canson)

CHALK
(Craf-T Products)

LIQUID PIGMENT PAINT
(Radiant Pearls by LuminArte)

PIGMENT POWDERS
(Perfect Pearls by Ranger)

ACRYLIC PAINT
(Making Memories)

METALLIC RUB-ONS
(Craf-T Products)

METALLIC WATERCOLOR PIGMENT PAINT
(Twinkling H$_2$Os by LuminArte)

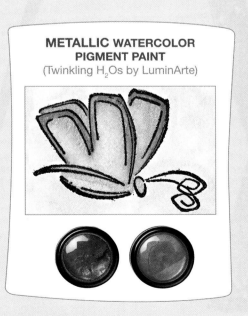

OUR
VALENTINE
SWEETHEART

ISABELLA
2002

Chapter 1

Accents and Embellishments

When diving into stamping for the first time, a good place to start is with page embellishments. Even simple stamped accents can give a page the finishing touch it needs. In this chapter you'll discover stamped accents colored with watercolor paint, postage-style stamped designs, stamping on pockets, different embossing techniques and much more. In addition, be inspired by step-by-step projects on:

Purrcel Post

CREATE FAUX POSTAGE-STAMP EMBELLISHMENTS

Kathi utilized stamped paw prints and cat images to create the look of postage stamps. She also used mailing tape from an old package on her photo mats and title to give the page a more authentic look. Punch out postage stamp shapes from tan cardstock using large and small punches. Stamp paw prints onto smaller shapes with red chalk ink. Stamp cancellation image over paw prints in black ink. Write the amount of postage in the lower right-hand corner with a red pen. Repeat process for larger cat stamps. Ink edges of all faux postage stamps with red chalk ink. Use black distressing ink to "muddy up" faux postage stamps and envelope.

Kathi Rerek, Scotch Plains, New Jersey

Supplies: *Cat and paw print stamps (Hero Arts); canceled postage stamp (Stampin' Up!); Nick Bantock Prussian Blue stamping ink and Tim Holtz Black Soot distress stamping ink (Ranger); Memories red chalk stamping ink (Stewart Superior); letter die cuts (QuicKutz); large and small postage stamp punches (McGill); patterned and solid cardstocks and vellum (Club Scrap); mailing tape; red pen*

TIP: When stamping an image, press the inked stamp straight down onto paper and lift the stamp straight up. If you rock the stamp or apply too much pressure, you could end up with a blurred image.

Country Life

PAIR COUNTRY-STYLE STAMPS WITH SEPIA PHOTOS AND VINTAGE IMAGES

Tractor and truck images add to the old-fashioned country look of Julie's page. Stamp images onto brown cardstock with brown chalk ink. Cut out images and ink edges with brown for an aged effect.

Julie Johnson, Seabrook, Texas

Supplies: *Truck stamps (River City Rubber Works); Colorbox brown chalk ink (Clearsnap); ribbon (Offray); letter charm (Card Connection); patterned paper (Wübie); rub-ons, photo holders, photo clips and brads (Making Memories); sugar mill sticker (source unknown); brown cardstocks; sandpaper*

Petroglyph

DECORATE A FOLD-OUT ELEMENT

A variety of petroglyph and texture stamps were the perfect accents for Oksanna's photos featuring actual prehistoric symbols. Using black ink, stamp petroglyphs on beige cardstock and tear edges. Accent images with gold dimensional paint. Stamp smaller symbols on small punched circles and bits of clay. To create fold-out element, cut two 8" squares from beige and tan cardstocks. Score and fold each into four equal squares and diagonally through the center. Attach photos to select quadrants and add texture stamps to others. Adhere top right quadrant of beige cardstock over bottom right quadrant of tan. Fold on all score lines to close the element and adhere to page background. Stamp front of fold-out with texture stamp and add a petroglyph image matted on tan cardstock.

Oksanna Pope, Los Gatos, California

Supplies: *Anthropomorph, Kokopelli, goat, mesh and crackle stamps, petroglyph stamp set and patterned papers (PSX Design); tan patterned paper (Bo-Bunny Press); sparkle spray, gold metallic dimensional paint and beads (Duncan); clay (Provo Craft); eyelets (C-Thru Ruler); decorative scissors (Fiskars); fibers (EK Success); letter stickers (Colorbök); beige and tan cardstocks; circle punch; black pen*

With great joy,
we announce the newest member of our family!

Nina Bernice Kniska
born October 1st, 2003, 10:27AM
weighing 8lbs, 3.5 ounces and 21 inches in length.

Andrew, MaryAnn and Drew Kniska

Supplies: *Rose and leaf stamps, pink and green stamping inks (Close To My Heart); letter stamps (PSX Design, Wordsworth); painted tags (The Embellished Girl); patterned paper (K & Company); metal corner accents and paper yarn (Making Memories); pink, white and yellow cardstocks; eyelets; ribbon*

Nina

STAMP BACKGROUND AND DETAILS IN MULTIPLE SHADES

Christi used a two-step stamping technique to create the rose and leaf accents at the corner of a birth announcement. The stamps are designed to go together, creating soft highlights for the detailed rose and leaf designs.

Christi Spadoni, Wrentham, Massachusetts

STEP-BY-STEP: TWO-STEP MULTICOLORED STAMPING

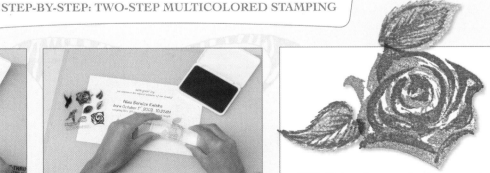

1 Mount stamps to clear acrylic blocks. In lighter shades of pink and green ink, stamp background leaves and rose designs.

2 Remove background stamps from acrylic blocks and attach finely detailed foreground stamps. Stamp detailed leaves and rose in darker shades of pink and green.

TIP: Using clear acrylic stamps and blocks allows for precise positioning when stamping over an image for a second time.

Hemingway's Cats

PAINT STAMPED IMAGES WITH WATERCOLORS

Lydia stamped cat and flower images on white cardstock, then colored each with watercolor paints to match certain elements of her vacation photos. Stamp images in black ink and paint each one. Lightly shade the face of each cat stamp with gray colored pencil. Once the paint dries, silhouette cut all images and apply crystal lacquer over them; let dry. After adhering flower stamps to corners, trim some of the petals so they do not exceed the borders of the page.

Lydia Rueger, Memory Makers Books

Supplies: *Watercolor paints (Staedtler); black stamping ink (Stamps by Judith); flower stamp (Outlines Rubber Stamp Co.); cat stamp (Hampton Art Stamps); crystal lacquer (Sakura Hobby Craft); letter die cuts (QuicKutz); teal, black and white cardstocks; colored pencil; black pen*

Spring Flowers

COLOR STAMPED IMAGES WITH CHALK

Beverly used chalk to add color to daffodil images. Stamp title onto pieces of cream cardstock using black ink. Place page pebbles over each letter. Accent torn edges of small cardstock squares with yellow chalk. Stamp daffodil images onto torn rectangular pieces of cardstock. Heat emboss with black embossing powder. Fill in inside of daffodils with chalk, using a blender pen to soften the colors. Outline torn edges of cardstock with yellow chalk.

Beverly Sizemore, Sulligent, Alabama

Supplies: *Letter stamps and black embossing powder (All Night Media); daffodil stamp (Rubber Stampede); black stamping inks (Clearsnap, Stampin' Up!); chalks (Stampin' Up!); blender pen and tag punch (EK Success); tag template (Accu-Cut); eyelets (Impress Rubber Stamps); metal phrase, page pebbles and eyelets (Making Memories); circle clips (Target); tan, cream and yellow cardstocks; foam tape*

You Stole Our Hearts

STAMP SIMPLE DESIGNS IN BLACK PAINT

Summer added drama to her stitched page by including designs stamped in black acrylic paint. Ink edges of red cardstock background with black ink. Trim pieces of white cardstock and ink edges with red and black inks. Stamp title on a small tag; ink edges with black and red inks. Using foam stamps, apply black paint and press onto page so that edges overlap photos, journaling and background.

Summer Ford, San Antonio, Texas

Supplies: *Letter stamps and black and red stamping inks (Stampin' Up!); foam stamps, date stamp, black acrylic paint and eyelet (Making Memories); red patterned paper (7 Gypsies); charm (Crafts Etc.); fibers; sewing machine; thread; red, white and black cardstocks; tag*

TIP: Before stamping and embossing on paper, vellum, tranparencies, plastic tiles or any other medium that may attract static, rub an anti-static pouch across the surface (available at stamp stores). Once embossing powder is poured over the image and the excess is removed, it will stick only to your image—there will be no stray particles sticking to your surface due to static cling.

Navy Pier

STAMP IMAGES ON A TRANSPARENCY

Lynne positioned stamped sun and compass images on her spread so they appear to be part of the background. Stamp images onto transparency using black solvent ink. Heat emboss with clear embossing powder. Cut out images and adhere to background. Cover parts of images with journaling and photos.

Lynne Rigazio Mau, Channahon, Illinois

Supplies: *Sun and compass stamps (Stampers Anonymous); nautical stamps, textured cardstocks and yellow patterned cardstock (Club Scrap); StazOn black stamping ink (Tsukineko); mushroom stamping ink (Ranger); embossing powder (JudiKins); metal letters and brads (Making Memories); metal rectangle rings and photo holders (7 Gypsies); label maker (Dymo); library pocket template (Deluxe Designs); globe nailhead (Magic Scraps); transparency*

TIP: Before stamping on metal, clean the surface with white vinegar or lemon juice to remove any residue.

Japanese Gardens

STAMP ON METAL, GLASS AND CORK

Shauna stamped accents on three different surfaces to add a bit of dimension to her page. Stamp Asian character onto metal tag with black solvent ink; set aside to dry. For stamping on glass, stamp the word "friend" onto small glass bottle with black solvent ink. Roll a piece of patterned paper and insert it in the bottle. Stamp "joy" character onto blue tag; ink edges. Insert brads in metal and paper tags and attach the two with string. Tie another string from metal tag to glass bottle. Adhere tags to page with foam tape and adhere bottle with glue dots. Stamp bamboo image onto cork with solvent ink; adhere to crumpled and inked paper with foam tape.

Shauna Berglund-Immel for
Hot Off The Press, Beaverton, Oregon

Supplies: *Patterned papers, preprinted words, cork sheet, glass bottle and tags (Hot Off The Press); letter stamps (Hero Arts); Asian character and word stamps (Inkadinkado); bamboo stamp (Rubber Stampede); StazOn and Brilliance black stamping inks (Tsukineko); white cardstock; brads; staples; foam tape*

Countless Hours Much Love

EMBOSS STENCIL LETTERS

Angelia used several layers of extra thick embossing powder on stencil letters to give a smooth, glossy appearance. Apply black ink to stencil letters. Sprinkle on extra thick embossing powder and heat from below. Repeat this process twice more while the stencil is still hot. Using black ink, stamp numbers and words on block of patterned paper and along left side of page. Layer embossed stencil letters over block of patterned paper with ribbon, charm, button and silk flower.

Angelia Wigginton, Belmont, Mississippi

Supplies: *Number and word stamps (Postmodern Design); stencil letters (Autumn Leaves); Versacolor black stamping ink (Tsukineko); extra thick embossing powder (Stampendous!); buttons (Junkitz); metal clock, heart charm and patterned papers (K & Company); date stamp, flowers and metal brads (Making Memories); ribbon (Me & My Big Ideas); black cardstock; vellum*

Just as the threads in the tapestry of our lifes are different so are the things we are thankful for. Only one thead remaines the same... Thankfulness to our Creator for the constant love he shows to us daily.

NOVEMBER

THANKFUL

Thankful

STAMP A VELLUM POCKET

Oksanna inserted reasons to be thankful into a vellum pocket that she decorated. Cut piece of vellum and stamp leaves on the front side. Flip vellum over and brush watered-down fabric paint on backside to add color. Attach vellum to page background with eyelets and thread fibers through eyelets. Insert journaled tags inside pocket.

Oksanna Pope, Los Gatos, California

Supplies: *Leaf stamps and patterned paper (PSX Design); fabric paint, metallic dimensional paint and sparkle spray (Duncan); fibers, metal letters and date (EK Success); "s" shaped paper clip (Making Memories); EZ2Cut tag template (Accu-Cut); brown and cream cardstocks; vellum; eyelets; colored pens*

Educational Options

INSERT JOURNALING IN A DECORATED POCKET

Jennifer accented a library-card pocket on this page by stamping with acrylic paints. Add acrylic paint to a stippling brush, dabbing off the excess. Lightly tap brush onto the surface of the stamps and press images on library pocket. Ink edges of pocket with black stamping ink. Insert journaling and photos accented with safety pins, ribbon and wire.

Jennifer S. Gallacher, Savannah, Georgia

Supplies: *Large stamp (Stamp Accents); checkered stamp (Stampin' Up!); Memories black stamping ink (Stewart Superior); black acrylic paint (Delta); patterned paper (7 Gypsies); tags (Avery); snaps, metal corner accent and wire (Making Memories); ribbon, safety pins, pink rub-ons and library-card pockets (Li'l Davis Designs); label maker (Dymo); green, pink and black cardstocks*

TIP: When adding colorants such as watercolor paint or markers to a black stamped outline, heat emboss the black outline first to prevent the lines from smearing when color is added.

8 is Great

DRESS UP A POCKET WITH SHIMMERING WATERCOLORS

An envelope Jodi decorated with stamps and shimmering watercolor paints allowed her room for more photographs and fit the playful birthday theme of the page. Create envelope using own pattern, ink edges with chalk ink and adhere folds. In black, stamp presents on front of envelope. When dry, color with shimmering watercolor paints. Stamp other presents in black and color with watercolors. Silhouette presents and position around page to coordinate with pocket.

Jodi Amidei, Memory Makers Books

Supplies: *Birthday present stamps (DeNami Design); letter stamps (PSX Design); Twinkling H₂Os watercolor paints (LuminArte); StazOn and Versafine black stamping inks (Tsukineko); Colorbox chalk ink (Clearsnap); patterned papers (Carolee's Creations, Cross My Heart); acrylic tags (Junkitz); ribbon (May Arts); orange, red and green cardstocks*

Supplies: *Christmas tree stamp and patterned paper (Wordsworth); sheet music stamp (Hero Arts); letter stamps (FontWerks); StazOn black stamping ink (Tsukineko); conchos (Scrapworks); buttons (Jesse James); red ribbon, snowflake eyelets and stocking charm (Making Memories); filigree corner accent (Boutique Trims); snaps (Chatterbox); white and black acrylic paints (Liquitex); green and white cardstocks; black pen; gold ribbon; slide mount; bleach*

All Decked Out

USE BLEACH INSTEAD OF STAMPING INK

Susan stamped her page title with letter stamps and acrylic paint, then used bleach to create the tree accent in the upper left-hand corner.

Susan Cyrus, Broken Arrow, Oklahoma

STEP-BY-STEP: STAMPING WITH BLEACH

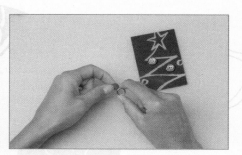

1 Cut rectangle from green cardstock that is similar in size to your stamp. Pour bleach onto paper towel and place on paper plate. Dab stamp on wet towel. Remove excess bleach by lightly blotting one time on a dry paper towel.

2 Place cardstock rectangle on dry paper towel. Press bleach-coated stamp onto cardstock. Bleached image will appear. Immediately wash stamp to prevent bleach from damaging rubber.

3 Insert buttons in conchos. Poke conchos through cardstock to decorate tree design.

Epcot

STAMP ON A CERAMIC TILE

Susan stamped a decorative pattern on a ceramic tile to create a Parisian feel on this page. Color rubber stamp with brick red permanent tile marker. Stamp the image onto the tile; let dry. Apply two layers of varnish and adhere over transparent image. Stamp border designs along edge of page using a foam stamp and green acrylic paint. Use the same paint to stamp title with letter stamps.

Susan Stringfellow, Cypress, Texas

Supplies: *Foam stamp and decorative brad (Making Memories); letter stamps (Wordsworth); pattern stamp (Anna Griffin); red brick tile marker, patterned and velveteen papers, ceramic tile, patterned transparency and fibers (www.thelittlescrapbookstore.com); green ribbon (Jo-Ann Fabrics); green acrylic paint; sage green cardstock; transparency*

Supplies: *Fern stamp (source unknown); shadow stamps (Hero Arts); striped stamp (Morning Star Stamp Company); black stamping inks (Stewart Superior, Tsukineko); Jungle Green stamping ink (Marvy); patterned papers (Scrap In A Snap); letter stickers (Creative Imaginations); fibers; green cardstock; circle clips; ribbon*

Fiddle Heads

PAIR FERN AND SHADOW STAMPS

LauraLinda stamped a tag and title block with fern and shadow stamps to enhance the botanical feel of this page. Stamp fern image in black ink on cardstock rectangle and tag. Using green ink, stamp different-sized shadow stamps around the edges of both page elements, allowing parts of the images to bleed off the paper. Repeat with striped stamp. Rub black ink pad along edges of cardstock and tag. Add letter and number stickers over ferns. Color circle clips with black solvent ink and add one to tag with fibers.

LauraLinda Rudy, Markham, Ontario, Canada

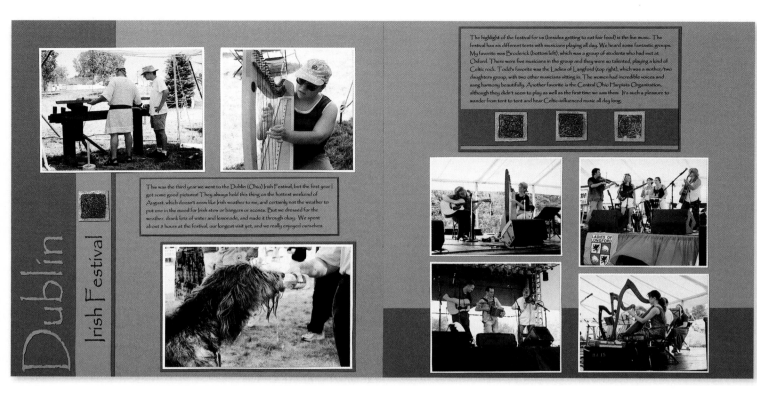

Dublin Irish Festival

STAMP INTO EXTRA THICK EMBOSSING POWDER

Janelle gave her page a Celtic look by creating faux metal embellishments. Her accents add interest to a simple page while keeping the focus on the photos and journaling.

Janelle Clark, Yorktown, Virginia

Supplies: *Celtic stamp (Stampa Rosa); Ultra Thick Embossing Enamel powder (Ranger); dimensional adhesive (JudiKins); Color-box silver and green stamping inks (Clearsnap); green and white cardstocks*

STEP-BY-STEP: FAUX METAL TILES

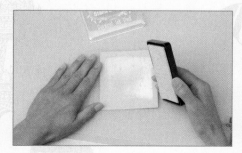

1 Wipe a silver ink pad across a piece of gray cardstock.

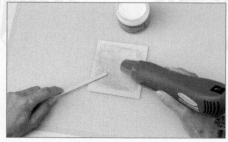

2 Pour extra thick embossing powder on silver ink. Heat with an embossing gun to melt. Repeat three times to create a thicker layer.

3 While final layer of embossing powder is still hot and soft, press stamp inked with green into it. Hold stamp on surface until powder has hardened slightly.

Tool Time

CREATE THE LOOK OF METAL EMBELLISHMENTS

On this page, Katie created stamped embellishments with silver extra thick embossing powder. Cut a strip of chipboard into three equal rectangles. Liberally apply watermark ink to cardboard by wiping across the inkpad several times. Sprinkle extra thick embossing powder onto chipboard and shake off excess. Melt with a heat gun. When substance cools, repeat two more times. Before the third layer cools and hardens, press tool stamps into it. Mat embellishments with red cardstock and adhere to page with foam tape.

Katie Swanson, South Milwaukee, Wisconsin

Supplies: *Letter stamps and black stamping ink (Stampin' Up!); tool stamps (Close To My Heart); Ultra Thick Embossing Enamel silver powder (Ranger); blue, gray, brown and red cardstocks; chipboard*

Build

CHANGE EMBELLISHMENTS' COLOR WITH EMBOSSING POWDER

Leslie heat embossed gold tool embellishments with silver powder so they would match the rest of her page. Brush tools with embossing ink. Sprinkle on silver embossing powder and heat. Adhere to cardstock rectangles, ink edges of rectangles and accent with screw snaps.

Leslie Herbert, Queen Creek, Arizona

Supplies: *Letter stamps (Hero Arts); Memories black stamping ink (Stewart Superior); embossing ink (Ranger); silver embossing powder (Close To My Heart); screw snaps (Making Memories); tool charms (www.memoriesoftherabbit.com); heat gun (Marvy); gray cardstocks*

Diane and Paul

EMBOSS ACCENTS ON VELLUM

For subtle, elegant accents on a wedding spread, Becky embossed flower stamps on vellum. Stamp vellum with flower images inked with watermark ink. Apply white embossing powder and heat. Repeat process for flower centers using silver embossing powder. Silhouette cut flowers from vellum and adhere across spread.

Becky Kent, Hilliard, Ohio
Photos: Angela Hampton, Durham, North Carolina

Supplies: *Daisy stamps and white embossing powder (Stampin' Up!); Versamark watermark stamping ink (Tsukineko); silver embossing powder (Ranger); letter die cuts (QuicKutz); decorative corner stickers (Stampendous!); patterned vellum (source unknown); silver, navy and white cardstocks; mulberry paper; vellum*

TIP: When adhering stamped and embossed vellum accents to your page, carefully apply adhesive under the embossed areas so it will not show through the vellum.

Bride/Groom

GLAZE A CLAY EMBELLISHMENT

Melissa stamped into clay, then added glaze to create a fitting accent for a wedding portrait. Stamp decorative image into moist clay with green chalk ink. Let clay harden and color hearts in the center of the design with a silver leafing pen. Coat with clear glaze for a glossy look. Outline image with silver leafing pen. Heat emboss torn edges of photo mat with silver embossing powder to coordinate.

Melissa Zeno, Westland, Michigan
Photo: Ben Arcenal, Canton, Michigan

Supplies: *Decorative stamp and heart punch (EK Success); Colorbox green chalk stamping ink (Clearsnap); dimensional glaze (JudiKins); silver embossing powder (Ranger); patterned vellum (Autumn Leaves); mini brads (Making Memories); silver leafing pen; air-dry clay; wire; sage, cream and burgundy cardstocks; vellum; brads; black pen*

Live

STAMP AND EMBOSS COIN HOLDERS

Laura stamped and embossed chipboard coin holders to use as embellishments in her title. Place coin holders over scrap paper. Randomly stamp top of coin holders with black and gray inks, allowing the pattern to bleed over the edges. Heat emboss with clear embossing powder.

Laura Stewart, Fort Wayne, Indiana

Supplies: *Stamp (Hero Arts); Ancient Page Coal Black and Stone Gray inks (Clearsnap); clear embossing powder (Ranger); coin holders (H.E. Harris); cross-stitch paper (Plaid); beads and jewelry hook (Westrim); love charm (www. accentology.com); metal letters (Making Memories); nailhead (Scrapworks); slide bracelet (Daffodil Hill); patterned paper (source unknown); black and white papers; black marker; cardstock; wire*

My Funny Valentine

EMBELLISH A PHOTO FRAME WITH STAMPED CLAY

Sande softened polymer clay by kneading it with her hands, and then fed it through a pasta machine to create a flat piece for her embellishment. After flattening red clay, use a template to cut out the shape. Stamp heart into red clay with black solvent ink. Using the same techniques above, flatten a cream piece of clay. Place the red clay shape on top of the cream piece and use it as a guide to cut a piece that is ¼" larger. Bake according to package directions, then coat with clear glaze. Stamp title and journaling on fabric with black solvent ink.

Sande Krieger, Salt Lake City, Utah

Supplies: *Letter stamps (Hero Arts, PSX Design); heart stamp (Stampin' Up!); StazOn black stamping ink (Tsukineko); fabric pouch and safety pins (Li'l Davis Designs); brads, leather frame and rub-ons (Making Memories); heart nailheads (Scrapworks); paper clip (EK Success); typewriter keys and linen (Jo-Ann Fabrics); ribbon (May Arts); "funny" letters (Foofala); heart charm (www.twopeasinabucket.com); black textured cardstock (Bazzill); toile patterned paper (Deluxe Designs); red script paper (7 Gypsies) polymer clay (Polyform Products); dimensional glaze (JudiKins); thread*

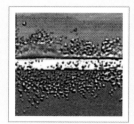

South Texas Snow

EMBELLISH WITH EMBOSSING POWDER

Linda used bronze extra thick embossing powder in various places on her page to give it a sandy look. Randomly dab clear embossing ink along edges of photos; apply bronze embossing powder and heat. Emboss title letters and edges of metal-rimmed tag to coordinate.

Linda Rodriguez, Corpus Christi, Texas

Supplies: *Ultra Thick Embossing Enamel bronze powder (Ranger); date stamp (Office Depot); Colorbox black stamping ink and clear embossing ink (Clearsnap); letter beads and jump ring (Westrim); metal-rimmed tag (Making Memories); blue and white cardstocks; embroidery floss*

I Am Me

USE CHILDREN'S HANDS AS STAMPS

Summer's children literally got their hands on this page, creating the perfect embellishments for a layout about their personalities. Apply blue and red inks to children's hands. Press hands onto vellum. Silhouette cut each hand and adhere to page background. Place journaling tag with children's photos over each one's corresponding handprint. Stamp date onto smaller vellum tag with black ink.

Summer Ford, San Antonio, Texas

Supplies: *Date stamp, metal letters and eyelets (Making Memories); blue, red and black stamping inks (Stampin' Up!); navy patterned paper (Daisy D's); striped patterned paper (Mustard Moon); fibers (Fibers By The Yard); vellum; white cardstock; embroidery floss; sewing machine; sandpaper*

TIP: When stamping the foot- or handprint of a very young child, bring the paper to his or her inked hand or foot rather than trying to stamp the hand or foot on the paper. This will result in a clearer image with less smearing.

St. Augustine

STAMP ON MICA

Lydia stamped on squares of mica to coordinate with the colors and textures of the garden door in her photo. Stamp on mica with purple ink, allowing stamp to bleed over the edges. Heat ink with embossing gun to avoid smearing. Mat mica on purple paper and adhere to page alongside decorative tiles. Repeat stamp above and below photograph to coordinate.

Lydia Rueger, Memory Makers Books

Supplies: *Leaf stamp (Magenta); Versacolor purple ink (Tsukineko); letter die cuts (QuickKutz); mica squares (Leave Memories); purple patterned paper (Club Scrap); tan patterned paper (Sonburn); decorative tiles and corners (EK Success); blue and purple cardstocks; purple pen*

Supplies: *Fleur-de-lis stamp (Rubber Stampede); Ancient Page black and Top Boss clear stamping inks (Clearsnap); evergreen embossing powder and perfect medium (Ranger); clear glue sticks (Duncan); letter stickers (Deluxe Designs); preprinted labels and patterned paper (Pebbles); mica (USArtQuest); snaps (Chatterbox); hook-and-eye fasteners (Prym-Dritz); fibers (Timeless Touches); star eyelet (Making Memories); black sticky strips (Therm O Web); green acrylic paint; sewing machine; olive cardstock; memorabilia; wire; teflon sheet; toothpick; black pen*

Love Letters From Paris

SEAL AN ENVELOPE WITH A FAUX WAX SEAL

Faux wax seals were the perfect complement for a heritage page featuring love letters from a soldier. Heidi used one to "seal" an envelope and three others as accents in the top right corner.

Heidi Schueller, Waukesha, Wisconsin

STEP-BY-STEP: FAUX WAX SEALS

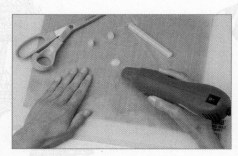

1 Cut small pieces from a hot glue stick and melt with a heat gun on a Teflon sheet.

2 Mix green acrylic paint with melted glue while still warm.

3 Heat glue again if necessary. Apply clear ink to stamp and press into glue. Hold stamp in place for several minutes.

As Good As It Gets

CREATE ICY EFFECTS WITH EMBOSSING POWDER

Summer made a snowflake out of extra thick embossing powder and a coffee filter to embellish this page. Fold a coffee filter until it is as small as possible. Use scissors to cut notches in random areas of the folded filter. Unfold the filter to reveal snowflake shape. Lightly rub navy blue ink over snowflake; let dry. Cover surface of snowflake with clear embossing ink, add extra thick embossing powder and heat. Repeat inking and embossing steps several times until desired thickness is achieved.

Summer Ford, San Antonio, Texas

Supplies: *Letter stamps (Hero Arts); navy stamping ink (Stampin' Up!); white stamping ink (Stewart Superior); Ultra Thick Embossing Enamel and white embossing powders (Ranger); metal letters, rub-on words and snowflake charm (Making Memories); fibers (Fibers By The Yard); patterned papers (Mustard Moon, Sweetwater); textured white paper (source unknown); navy cardstock; sewing machine; coffee filters*

TIP: When stamping on nonporous surfaces such as mica, glass or plastic, use solvent ink for best results. If using other ink types, heat the ink with an embossing gun or emboss with powder to keep the image from smearing.

Autumn Treasures

CREATE PATTERNS ON MICA

Andrea used thin layers of mica stamped with leaf images to coordinate with her deep textured background. Stamp leaves on mica with clear embossing ink and brush with copper pigment powder. Stamp titles and names in embossing ink and emboss with black embossing powder. Spray mica, title, and name blocks with protectant spray to seal.

Andrea Lyn Vetten-Marley, Aurora, Colorado

Supplies: *Leaf stamp (Northwoods Rubber Stamps); letter stamps (Stampabilities); quote stamp (PSX Design); clear embossing ink (Tsukineko); black embossing powder (Ranger); protectant spray (Caroline's); textured cardstocks (Provo Craft); Pearl Ex pigment powders (Jacquard Products); copper cardstock; mica; date stamp; fibers*

Dance Like No One Is Watching

STAMP AND EMBOSS ON MICA

A jagged sheet of mica that Melissa stamped gives her card added interest. Bronze embossing powder applied around the edges gives it a finishing touch.

Melissa Smith, North Richland, Texas

Supplies: *Phrase stamp and beads (Leave Memories); dress stamp (Inkadinkado); StazOn black and Versamark clear stamping inks (Tsukineko); Ultra Thick Embossing Enamel bronze powder (Ranger); mica sheets (USArtQuest); handmade patterned papers (Creative Papers Online Handmade Paper); brown and olive cardstocks*

STEP-BY-STEP: STAMPING AND EMBOSSING MICA

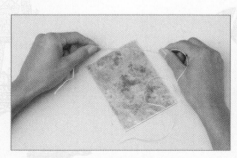

1 Separate layers of mica with dental floss until you have a thinner, translucent piece.

2 Break edges of mica as desired until the piece is jagged on sides.

3 Stamp image onto mica using black solvent ink. Apply embossing ink to jagged edges, sprinkle with bronze extra thick embossing powder and heat emboss edges.

Merry Christmas

COLOR HOLIDAY IMAGES WITH MARKERS

Gold accents paired with traditional holiday colors make the perfect Christmas card. Stamp all images with clear embossing ink. Pour on gold embossing powder and heat. Color inside each gold outline with markers.

Eva Marie Kreil, Memory Makers Executive Assistant

Supplies: *Holiday stamp (DeNami Design); colored markers (American Tombow); cream, green and burgundy cardstocks; deckle scissors; gold ribbon*

TIP: When dipping an object into melted embossing powder, hold it with tweezers or small tongs. After dipping, place the object on a nonstick heat-resistant surface, such as a Teflon sheet, waxed paper or aluminum foil.

Live in the Moment

USE A COMPACT DISC

Gemiel used a CD dipped in extra thick embossing powder to give this card an interesting twist. Stamp phrase onto a piece of a broken CD with black StazOn ink; let dry. Pour extra thick embossing powder into a Melting Pot heating device and heat until melted. Mix dye into the melted substance. Dip CD into extra thick embossing powder. Press tiny glass marbles into the CD's edge while still warm.

Gemiel Matthews, Yorktown, Virginia

Supplies: *Phrase stamp (Inkadinkado); black StazOn stamping ink (Tsukineko); Ultra Thick Embossing Enamel powder, To Dye For UTEE dye and Melting Pot (Ranger); patterned paper and watch face (7 Gypsies); black cardstock; clock hands (Walnut Hollow); tiny glass marbles (Halcraft); brads (Making Memories); fibers (Fibers By The Yard); vellum phrase (Jo-Ann Fabrics); compact disc*

If the Shoe Fits

STAMP ON LAMINATE CHIPS

Kari gave this card a funky look by using shoe stamps and retro patterned paper. Stamp shoe images with black solvent ink onto laminate chips at jaunty angles. Tie gingham ribbon through each chip and adhere to card with foam tape.

Kari Hansen-Daffin, Memory Makers magazine

Supplies: *Shoe stamps (Inkadinkado); black StazOn stamping ink (Tsukineko); patterned paper and acrylic alphabet stickers (Creative Imaginations); red patterned paper (Cross My Heart); ribbon (Jo-Ann Fabrics); vellum; black cardstock; brads; foam tape; laminate chips; black marker*

Supplies: *Vine and berry stamps, Blue Frost spectrum stamping ink, Winter White embossing powder and heat gun (Stampin' Up!); VersaMark clear embossing stamping ink (Tsukineko); brayer (Speedball); white mulberry paper; blue cardstocks; eyelets; fibers; water bottle; paper towels*

Card with Blue Doors

TRY A RESIST TECHNIQUE

Inking over stamped and embossed images allowed Tara to give this card a soft, watercolored look while displaying a unique resist technique.

Tara Bazata, Thornton, Colorado

STEP-BY-STEP: EMBOSSED RESIST TECHNIQUE

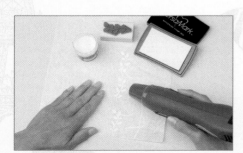

1 Stamp images on mulberry paper with watermark ink. Apply white embossing powder and heat.

2 Cut out stamped section from mulberry paper and place on scrap paper. With a brayer, roll blue ink over entire stamped piece.

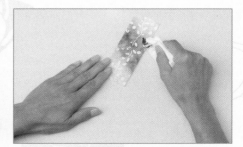

3 Spray stamped piece with water to make ink bleed and dab ink away from embossed design with a tissue. Repeat steps for second "door" of card and adhere to white cardstock.

Miss You

STAMP WITH BLEACH

Torrey stamped the face and images on this cat-shaped card using bleach instead of ink. Cut purple cardstock into cat shape. Stamp cat's face onto cardstock using a bleach-soaked paper towel (see technique on page 22). Repeat this process on the cat's body using various heart stamps. Stamp heart outline onto darker purple cardstock. Stamp "miss you" inside heart. Cut out heart using deckle scissors and adhere to cat. Adorn with heart brads and fibers.

Torrey Miller, Thornton, Colorado

Supplies: *Cat face stamp (Stampendous!); music heart stamp (Stampa Rosa); fractured heart stamp (Magenta); outline heart stamp and swirl heart stamp (Hero Arts); solid mini heart mini stamp (Close To My Heart); stitched heart stamp (Heart Patch Craft); miss you stamp (EK Success); VersaMagic stamping ink (Tsukineko); heart brads (Creative Impressions); fibers (Fiber Scraps); purple cardstocks; bleach*

Thank You

ADD STAMPING TO SERENDIPITY SQUARES

Nancy stamped on serendipity squares to give this card an eclectic look. Stamp on yellow, green, blue and red cardstocks with small script stamps. Cut pieces and strips from all colors and layer on ¼" squares of yellow cardstock. Accent with chalk inks, green glitter glue, mirror, gems and nailhead. Double mat squares using blue, green, yellow, and brown cardstocks. Stamp "thank you" onto a small piece of yellow cardstock using black ink; heat emboss. Ink edges with blue chalk ink and adhere to card.

Nancy Walker, Nashville, Tennessee

Supplies: *Script stamps (Club Scrap, Hero Arts, PSX Design); stamping inks (Clearsnap, Ranger, Stewart Superior); embossing powder and green glitter glue (Ranger); star (Buttons Galore); mirror, gems and nailhead (JewelCraft); colored cardstocks*

Thanks for...

COLOR WITH CHALKS

Suzanne colored the tulips on this card with chalks that match her cardstock background perfectly. Stamp tulip image onto cream cardstock with black ink. Stamp phrase using lavender ink. Chalk tulips and stems with purple and green. Mat stamped image on torn green cardstock and mount on purple card.

Suzanne Brooksbank, Aliso Viejo, California

Supplies: *Tulip stamp, phrase stamp, black and lavender stamping inks (Stampin' Up!); cream, green, and lavender cardstocks; colored chalk*

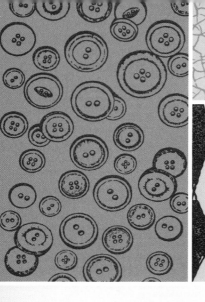

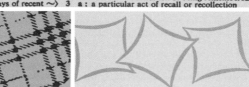

MOMENTS

mem·o·rize \'mem-ə-,rīz\ vt -rized; -riz·ing (ca. 1838) : to commit to
memory : learn by heart — mem·o·riz·able \-,rī-zə-bəl\ adj — mem·o-
ri·za·tion \,mem-(ə-)r 'zā-shən\ n — mem·o·riz·er n MF memoire, fr
memoria, fr. memo
mora delay, Gk me
e the power or pr
arned and retained esp. through associative mechanisms b : the
store of things learned and retained from an organism's activity or
experience as evidenced by modification of structure or behavior or by
recall and recognition 2 a: commemorative remembrance ⟨erected a
statue in ~ of the hero⟩ b : the fact or condition of being remembered
⟨days of recent ~⟩ 3 a : a particular act of recall or recollection

TOO BIG

RON JR

MAY 2004

When Daddy asked you to get his swimming trunks, you decided to try them on for size...
NOPE! They didn't fit. They were obviously TOO BIG!

There will be a time when you finally grow into a pair that size.
But for now, I'm thankful that they DON'T FIT because I'm enjoying you
just the way you are right now...my silly, nutty, sweet LITTLE boy!

Chapter
Backgrounds

When you create page backgrounds with stamps, you lay the foundation for your entire design. Browse through a plethora of background ideas including ones with distressing, iridescent pigment powders, block stamping and woven stamped strips. Discover more ideas through step-by-step examples of:

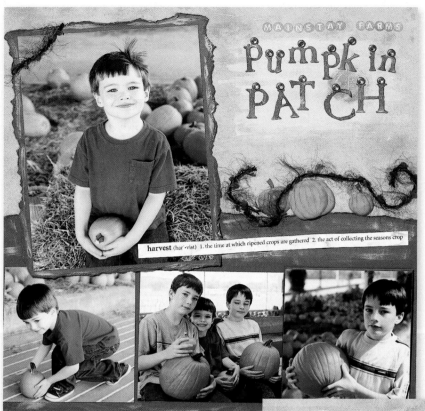

Pumpkin Patch

SHADE WATERMARK IMAGES WITH CHALK

With fields of pumpkins in her photos, K'Lynne created a background of delicately shaded pumpkins. Stamp pumpkins on background paper with watermark ink. To highlight the images, gently apply brown chalk to the wet ink. Using white paint and a "dry brush" technique—a dry paintbrush with very little paint—accent the background paper.

K'Lynne Dunham, Cleburne, Texas

Supplies: *Orange patterned paper (Provo Craft); Fall Fun stamp set, Really Rust ink and clear embossing powder (Stampin' Up!); VersaMark watermark ink (Tsukineko); brown chalk, photo holders, metal word, metal letter charms and definition stickers (Making Memories); letter stamps (PSX Design); FIMO orange clay (Eberhard Faber); fibers (Fibers By The Yard); peach pen; white acrylic paint; brown cardstock; eyelets; sandpaper*

TIP: Be aware that different types of inks behave differently when stamped on different types of papers. An ink that dries well on cardstock may smear on vellum or glossy paper. Experiment with your ink to determine whether it needs to be heat set or embossed on the paper you are using.

All Boy

USE WORD AND NUMBER STAMPS TO CREATE A BACKGROUND

Choosing various stamps from a set, Lara created an interesting background of numbers and words. Stamp down one side of page background with brown ink, lining up the stamps as you progress and fitting different ones next to each other. Fill ¼ of the background. Use one ink color to keep the background unified.

Lara Scott, Draper, Utah

Supplies: *Van Dyke Brown stamping ink (Ranger); Rough Estimate stamp sheet (Ma Vinci's); swirl patterned paper (Club Scrap); key and keyhole stickers and "A" letter tag (EK Success); page pebbles (Magic Scraps); bottle cap letter (Li'l Davis Designs); "L" metal letter and rub-on letters (Making Memories); metal letter tag (DieCuts with a View); letter page pebble (Creative Imaginations); green and blue cardstocks; vellum*

Soap Mohawk

EDGE A PAGE WITH AN INK PAD

Becky used an ink pad to grunge up the edges of her background and other page elements. Cut a thin strip and a large wavy-edged piece from shades of orange cardstock. Using a "direct to paper" technique, wipe a blue ink pad along the edges of background, strip, wavy edges and journaling block.

Becky Kent, Hilliard, Ohio

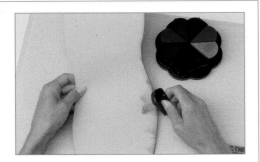

TIP: Simply brush an ink pad along edges of cardstock, vertically or horizontally, for added detail. Inking textured cardstock will add even more visual dimension to your page.

Supplies: *Adirondack Denim stamping ink (Ranger); letter die cuts (QuicKutz); white rub-on letters (Making Memories); shades of orange and blue textured cardstocks (Bazzill); circle cutter (Creative Memories); eyelets; white pen*

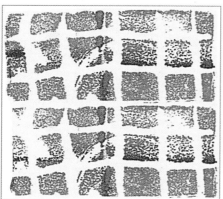

A Father's Love

CREATE YOUR OWN BACKGROUND STAMP

Julie says to create your own stamp, you can "use anything to make a design in Styrofoam, such as a rubber stamp, shaped brads, eyelets or even an apple slicer." For the background stamp used on this spread, she cut a piece of flat foam from a tray and made a design with an embossing stylus.

Julie Geiger, Gold Canyon, Arizona

Supplies: *Fantasy three-color stamp pad (Rubber Stampede); foam letter stamps (Making Memories); words stamp (PSX Design); StazOn black solvent ink (Tsukineko); clear embossing ink and clear Ultra Thick Embossing Enamel powder (Ranger); dimensional glaze (JudiKins); ceramic tile (Home Depot); black, white and turquoise papers; tiny glass marbles; foam tray; dry embossing stylus; eyelets; black gingham ribbon; baby wipes*

STEP-BY-STEP: HANDMADE FOAM STAMPS

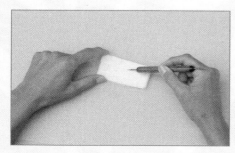

1. Cut a small rectangle from a thin foam tray. Use an embossing stylus to create deep ridges in foam in a checkerboard pattern.

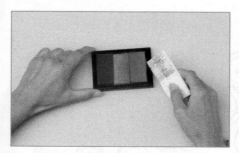

2. Apply ink to foam rectangle from a multi-colored ink pad.

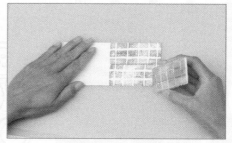

3. Stamp inked foam piece on white cardstock. The pattern carved into the foam will transfer onto cardstock to form a unique background design.

Delight in the Little Things

STAMP A COLOR-BLOCKED BACKGROUND

Janetta stamped blocks of brightly colored paper for a color-blocked design. Stamp insect images with black ink on two blocks and flower images with watermark ink on the other two. Sprinkle flowers with pink and black embossing powders; heat to set. To complete the page, frame the blocks with black cardstock.

Janetta Abucejo Wieneke, Memory Makers Books
Photo: Johanna Paluda, Westminster, Colorado

Supplies: *Butterfly, dragonfly and letter stamps (My Sentiments Exactly); tulip foam stamp and black embossing powder (Plaid); flower foam stamp (source unknown); Vivid black stamping ink (Clearsnap); VersaMark watermark ink and pink embossing powder (Tsukineko); lowercase letter stamps and word stamps (Hero Arts); corner buttons (Jesse James); eyelets; black, white, hot pink and green cardstocks*

Childhood

STAMP CHARACTERS ON A BACKGROUND

Teddi randomly stamped retro girl images across her background. Place 8½ x 11" pink cardstock over scrap paper. Stamp images, allowing some to flow off the edges. To create the borders, stamp one image on each strip, sprinkle with clear embossing powder and heat.

Teddi Lynn Von Pingel, Mesa, Arizona

Supplies: *EZ Mount Retro Ad Art stamps (Sunday International); Colorbox black stamping ink (Clearsnap); label maker stickers (Pebbles); date stamp (Making Memories); hot pink and black cardstocks; clear embossing powder; black pen*

How a Mother Is Measured

MASK A PHOTO TO STAMP A BACKGROUND

To create a crackle background around her mother's profile, Lisa began by scanning the original photo at high resolution and printing it on textured cardstock. To coordinate, she added the same crackle stamp to other areas of the spread.

Lisa Jobson, Ajax, Ontario, Canada
Photo: Sears Portrait Studio, Brampton, Ontario, Canada

Supplies: Heart patterned paper (The Paper Co.); newsprint patterned paper (7 Gypsies); paint patterned paper (Karen Foster Design); Italy paper (Outdoors and More); Crackle, Calligraphy Invitation and Williamsburg Shell stamps (PSX Design): Cosmic Copper stamping ink (Tsukineko); typewriter letter stickers (EK Success); page pebble letters and metal letter charms (Making Memories); Blue Topaz metallic paint (Plaid); Rich Gold paint (Jo Sonja's); Moments charm (Card Connection); foam Fleur de Lis Chunky Stamp (Duncan); white, cream, taupe and pale blue cardstocks; blue measuring tape; gold photo corners; metal label holder; jump rings; silk flowers; staples; blue pen

STEP-BY-STEP: MASKING AROUND A PHOTOGRAPH

1 Photocopy photo in black-and-white on plain copy paper. Silhouette cut subject from photocopy.

2 Place silhouetted photocopy directly over your photo's subject. Apply copper metallic ink to crackle patterned stamp. Stamp across background. Remove photocopy to reveal stamping around subject's face only.

Family 1945

USE A WATER BRUSH TO COLOR A BACKGROUND

Nancy chose a romantic floral stamp to create a custom background for her French bulletin board-style page. Stamp flowers with black ink in rows, starting at the bottom and aligning the images as you move upward. Before coloring the images, transfer small portions of stamping ink to the ink pad's lid by squeezing the pad and the lid together. Use a water brush to pick up ink from the lid and color the flowers.

Nancy Kliewer, Fairfax, Virginia

Supplies: *Toile Blossoms, Antique Cracking and word stamps, water pen, black, Creamy Caramel, Forest Foliage, Garden Green, Rose Red and Rose Romance stamping inks (Stampin' Up!); fibers (Me & My Big Ideas); buttons (Daisy D's); yellow, hot pink and tan cardstocks; pink ribbon*

TIP: To change colors when applying multiple shades of ink with a water brush, scribble the pen on scratch paper until the color is no longer visible.

Family Memories

CREATE A MONOCHROMATIC BACKGROUND

Using several flower stamps from a set, Janelle stamped with an ink color that strengthened the page's monochromatic hues. Stamp with tan inks on blocks of white and beige papers. For an embellishment, stamp one of the flowers with watermark ink and emboss with gold powder.

Janelle Clark, Yorktown, Virginia

Supplies: *Country Wildflowers stamp set (Hero Arts); Ancient Page Sandalwood ink (Clearsnap); VersaMark watermark ink (Tsukineko); gold embossing powder; gold textured paper; cream, brown, taupe, white and gold cardstocks; brown pen*

Tis the Season

DISTRESS BACKGROUND PAPER

Cindy created a background that resembled her distressed sticker embellishments. Spritz red and green papers with water and apply watered-down brown acrylic paint. Crumple papers and flatten to dry. Tear edges of papers and wipe a black ink pad over the papers for a distressed look. Adhere red and green papers to background and ink around edges of layout.

Cindy Harris, Modesto, California
Photo: JC Penney, Modesto, California

Supplies: *Christmas and label stickers and red patterned paper (Pebbles); black stamping ink (Stampendous!); white, tan and green cardstocks; brown acrylic paint; gingham ribbon; brads; paper clip; wire; beads; foam tape*

Springtime Is Happiness

COVER A BACKGROUND WITH WORD STAMPS

Julie stamped a background on her entire 12 x 12" spread. Use a sponge brush to apply a light layer of acrylic paint to a word stamp; press it onto background. Continue the process to fill the spread and let dry. Layer photos and journaling over painted areas.

Julie Johnson, Seabrook, Texas

Supplies: *White paint (Plaid); words stamp (American Art Stamp); white rub-ons, metal phrase and page pebble (Making Memories); square punch; blue and terra cotta cardstocks; sponge paint brush; ribbon*

Someday You'll Be...

SMUDGE INK PADS FOR ADDED BACKGROUND COLOR

Linda used various ink colors as a backdrop to her title. Print title on vellum; tear right side. Choose red, green and gold stamping inks and smudge them in horizontal strips over the title. Brush journaling strips with colored ink as well to coordinate with the title's background. For border and frame, apply pigment paint to torn cardstock strips and assemble.

Linda Rodriguez, Corpus Christi, Texas

Supplies: *Fresco brown, orange and green stamping inks (Stampa Rosa); gold frame (Hirschberg Schutz & Co.); fibers (Rubba Dub Dub); Radiant Pearls pigment paint (Lumin-Arte); dark blue and white cardstocks; brads; black pen; vellum*

Fall

USE FOAM STAMPS TO ENHANCE OTHER PATTERNS

After designing a color-blocked background with cardstock, various patterned papers and fabric, Adrienne stamped one of the blocks to coordinate. Load a foam stamp with a thin layer of rust-colored acrylic paint. Stamp flower images on the forest green section of patterned background paper, allowing parts of the stamps to bleed over the edges. Assemble with other background elements.

Adrienne Lehtinen, Portsmouth, Virginia

Supplies: *Patterned papers (Chatterbox, Rusty Pickle); floral foam stamp set, craft metal, red, green and yellow acrylic paints (Making Memories); letter stickers (Creative Imaginations); skeleton leaf (Stampin' Up!); label maker (Dymo); rust and olive cardstocks; transparency; brads; fibers; leather; wooden tag; paper tag; fabric*

Supplies: *Patterned paper (Creative Imaginations); VersaMark watermark ink (Tsukineko); Peridot embossing powder (Stampendous!); clear Ultra Thick Embossing Enamel powder (Ranger); blue and green re-inkers (Stampa Rosa); glass bottle (Leave Memories); gold twine; shells; mini starfish; sand; fibers; computer printed photo corners; brads; transparency*

TIP: To tear a transparency sheet, cut into one side with scissors first to get the tear started.

The Sea

EMBOSS A TRANSPARENCY TO RESEMBLE WATER

Melissa used extra thick embossing powder to create a wet effect on a transparency. She tore the upper and lower edges of the transparency and embossed with gold powder for an extra touch.

Melissa Smith, Seabrook, Texas

STEP-BY-STEP: EXTRA THICK EMBOSSING POWDER ON TRANSPARENCIES

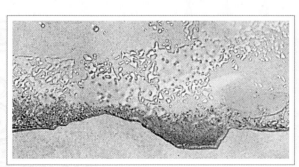

1 To create the look of water, apply clear watermark ink randomly to a transparency sheet. Sprinkle extra thick embossing powder on the sheet and heat with an embossing gun.

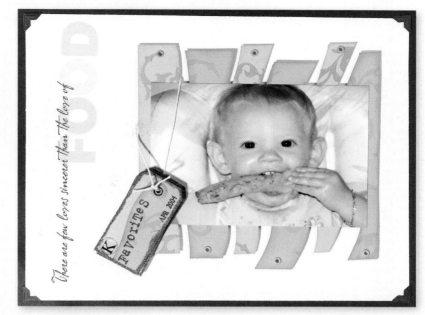

Supplies: *Letter stickers (Mrs. Grossman's); pattern, letter and date stamps (Making Memories); black stamping ink (Hampton Arts Stamps); Apple Barrel lavender and turquoise acrylic paints (Plaid); letter sticker (source unknown); page pebble; purple glitter; embossing powder; black, white, lavender and turquoise cardstocks; photo corners; eyelets; twine; snap*

The Love of Food

INCLUDE STAMPED STRIPS FOR A PLAYFUL BACKGROUND

Saralyn pulled colors from her photo to create a fun background design. Cut wavy strips from cardstock using a craft knife and cutting mat. To make sure the pieces fit together, cut complementary curves while alternating the colors, progressing from left to right. Use coordinating ink colors to shade the edges of each strip. Mount strips to white cardstock with foam tape and place photo on top.

Saralyn Berkowitz, Long Beach, New York

Stormy Maui

LAYER STAMPED AND EMBOSSED IMAGES

Sandra's dark, layered background sets the mood for photos of a stormy day. Use watermark ink to stamp words, fern and shell images on background. Emboss with clear powder. Stamp more images with metallic ink and emboss again. For more sparkle and texture, drop liquid ink on the page, blot the drops and emboss with gold and copper powders. Adhere tulle over background with translucent embossing paste. Stamp and emboss additional shell images on another piece of cardstock, silhouette cut and place over and under tulle.

Sandra Aoyagi, Honolulu, Hawaii

Supplies: *Shell, fern and letter stamps, sparkle embossing powder and brown stamping ink (Hero Arts); Brilliance Mineral three-color stamping ink, VersaColor Green Tea and stamping inks (Tsukineko); translucent embossing paste (Dreamweaver Stencils); metal letters (Colorbök); script patterned paper (source unknown); black and white cardstocks; photo corners; tulle*

Girl Power

STAMP AND DYE MULBERRY PAPER

Rebecca created a tie-dye effect by stamping and embossing images on mulberry paper, then adding liquid inks to color the background.

Rebecca Chabot, Sanford, Maine

Supplies: *Daisy and dragonfly unmounted stamps (The Angel Company); Lilac Luster embossing powder, clear embossing powder, Perfect Plum and Lavender Lace Classic liquid stamping ink (Stampin' Up!); Indigo Blue, Aquamarine and Mulberry liquid stamping ink and silver stamping ink (Tsukineko); pewter label holders (Making Memories); flower and peace charms (Keepsake Designs); white stamping ink; mulberry paper; purple, baby blue and periwinkle cardstocks; silver brads; silver pen; hand-sewing needle; purple thread and fibers; spray bottle; rubber gloves*

STEP-BY-STEP: TIE-DYED BATIK TECHNIQUE

1 Stamp images in mulberry paper and emboss with white powder. Lay sheet on a tray and mist entire sheet with water.

2 Randomly squirt blue liquid stamping ink across wet paper. Spread ink around with a gloved hand. Repeat with purple ink, allowing the colors to blend together.

3 Place sheet on newspaper and let dry.

Epcot 1998

SWIPE INK PADS ON WATER-COLOR PAPER

The background of Pam's journaling strips and photo mat draw attention due to direct-to-paper inking on watercolor paper. The paper's texture results in an interesting effect. Tear strips of paper and add journaling with letter stamps and black ink. Wipe blue and green ink pads across the strips, allowing the colors to overlap. Tear larger piece of paper for photo mat and ink with the same colors.

Pam Canavan, Clermont, Florida
Photo: Wendy Van Order

Supplies: *Patterned paper (Wordsworth); watercolor paper (Strathmore); blue, green and black stamping inks (Close To My Heart); slide mounts (Loersch); letter stamps (Hero Arts); blue paint (Delta)*

My Friend My Inspiration

COMBINE MANY STAMPS ON A TORN BACKGROUND

Holle wanted to experiment with layering various stamps and ink types to create an intricate background design. Tear a piece of navy cardstock in half diagonally. Stamp various images onto navy cardstock with chalk inks. Overlap with images in other colors next; stamp images in metallic inks last. Ink torn edges of photo mats with brown to coordinate.

Holle Wiktorek, Reunion, Colorado

Supplies: *Letter stamps (Hero Arts, LaPluma, Postmodern Design, PSX Design); various background stamps (Stampendous!); blue patterned paper (Frances Meyer); Colorbox chalk stamping inks (Clearsnap); metallic stamping inks (Tsukineko); cork sheet (Creative Impressions); metal frame, wood frame, clay phrase and bubble word (Li'l Davis Designs); dark blue, medium blue, light blue and tan cardstocks; green vellum; star brads*

Dream

WEAVE CONTRASTING STAMPED CARDSTOCKS

Silver embossing on Andrea's woven background coordinates well with her black-and-white photographs. Using watermark ink, impress a large word and phrase stamp across sheets of dark purple and lavender 12 x 12" cardstock. Emboss with silver powder. Cut 12⅓" strips of purple cardstock horizontally and 12⅓" strips of lavender cardstock vertically. Weave purple strips over and under lavender strips to form a 12 x 12" piece. Trim edges and adhere to sheets of lavender and purple cardstocks. Stamp, emboss and weave a smaller piece to mat a stamped butterfly.

Andrea Lyn Vetten-Marley, Aurora, Colorado

Supplies: *Letter stamps (Making Memories, Wordsworth); word and phrase stamp (PSX Design); butterfly stamp (DeNami Design); VersaMark watermark ink (Tsukineko); silver embossing powder (Ranger); white mulberry paper; ribbon (Offray); dark purple and lavender cardstocks; vellum; foam tape*

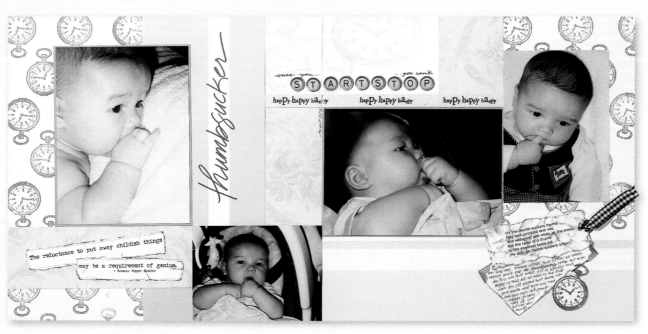

Thumbsucker

SCAN A STAMPED IMAGE

Kah-Mei stamped a pocket watch repeatedly across parts of her background, then scanned them for a different effect in the center of her spread. Stamp watches in rows across white cardstock using brown ink. To cover the cardstock evenly, rotate the stamp 180 degrees for each new row. Scan several images, enlarge on the computer and print out. Cut the stamped paper and scanned images and adhere over sections of patterned background.

Kah-Mei Smith, Coquitlam, British Columbia, Canada

Supplies: *Patterned papers (Anna Griffin, SEI); pocket watch stamp and Chocolate Brown stamping ink (Rubber Stampede); clear Ultra Thick Embossing Enamel powder (Ranger); typewriter key stickers (EK Success); twill tape (7 Gypsies); gingham ribbon (Offray); tan and white cardstocks; gold photo corner; black and brown pens*

Have Yourself a...

COORDINATE PAGE ELEMENTS WITH STAMPING

Using one stamp, Janelle enhanced patterned paper and created a matching tag. Use black ink to stamp holly sprigs randomly on green patterned paper. Tear off top half and color edge with gold leafing pen. Adhere to red background. Stamp image in black again around edges of tag. Shade with watercolor pencils and a blender pen. In green ink, stamp phrase in the center of tag.

Janelle Clark, Yorktown, Virginia
Photos: Kristina Smith, Leetonia, Ohio

Supplies: *Green patterned paper (Karen Foster Design); holly stamp (Sugarloaf Products); phrase stamp (Inkadinkado); Ancient Page black and green stamping inks (Clearsnap); green and red watercolor pencils (Derwent); gold leafing pen (Krylon); red paper yarn (Making Memories); heart buttons (Stamp Doctor); green, white, gold and red cardstocks; blender pen; wire*

Five Years

CREATE A SUBTLE STAMPED AND INKED BACKGROUND

Summer created a color-blocked background, stamping and inking certain areas for interest. Stamp a leaf design around edges of green cardstock background with green ink, allowing the design to bleed over the edges. Cut apart white embossed leaf paper and brush design with green ink. Adhere pieces across background; layer with green mulberry paper. To coordinate, stamp and emboss titles and tags using the same green ink.

Summer Ford, San Antonio, Texas

Supplies: *Toile leaf stamp (Stampabilities); patterned papers (Chatterbox); embossed leaf paper (Lasting Impressions); tin tiles, metal-rimmed heart tags and metal number (Making Memories); letter stamps and Mellow Moss stamping ink (Stampin' Up!); Moss embossing powder (Ranger); slide mount (Magic Scraps); number stamps (Hero Arts); blue cardstock; green mulberry paper; vellum; buttons; fibers; ribbons; sandpaper; cheesecloth*

Jeanne and Charlene Willardson, Ca. 1948, San Diego, California One of Mom's favorite pictures of her two girls. Mom remembered that Jeanne was always the "little mother" to Charlene, who in turn was the "little mother" to Doug and Rodney.

Charlene and Jeanne Willardson Ca. 1948, San Diego, California Charlene remembered: "There's big sister always trying to make me do what I was supposed to do. (Did she *ever* succeed?)" I guess the mothering instinct comes out early in all little girls.

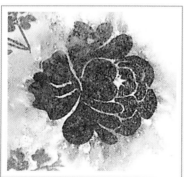

Sisters

SPRITZ STAMPED IMAGES FOR A WATER-WEBBED LOOK

Jeanne gave her stamped background a watercolor painting effect by using a technique she calls water webbing.

Jeanne Pittman, San Diego, California

Supplies: *Rose and Maidenhair stamps (Stars & Stamps Forever); Royal Satin Kaleidoscope stamping ink (Tsukineko); letters stamps (Close To My Heart); heart and key charms (Fancifuls); colored pencils (Sanford); heavy white cardstock (Fox River Paper); burgundy, green, navy and white cardstocks; spray bottle; burgundy thread; red pen*

STEP-BY-STEP: WATER WEBBING

1 Using multicolored ink pads in shades of green and purple, stamp one flower and greenery.

2 Mist wet ink with water immediately. Ink colors will spread out from the images.

3 Continue to stamp flowers and greenery one at a time. Mist each one with water while ink is still wet, until background in finished.

Supplies: *Stickers, patterned paper and vellum (American Crafts); snowflake and letter stamps (PSX Design); VersaMark watermark ink (Tsukineko); Colorbox black and lavender stamping inks (Clearsnap); rub-on letters (Making Memories); seed beads (Beadworks); lavender, purple, orange and green cardstocks; black pen*

Come Out and Play

CREATE A DELICATE BACKGROUND WITH WATERMARK INK

Subtle watermarked images create a good balance with bright cardstocks and patterned papers. Ink a snowflake stamp with watermark ink and randomly press onto lavender cardstock. This ink deepens the paper's color for a tone-on-tone effect. Cut pieces of purple cardstock, patterned paper and strips of patterned vellum and layer over parts of the watermarked background.

Kah-Mei Smith, Coquitlam, British Columbia, Canada

Hippo Tipping

INK CRUMPLED CARDSTOCK FOR A MASCULINE LOOK

Amy used an ink pad to enhance a rugged look for her layout. Crumple green cardstock and flatten it out. Use a black ink pad to wipe evenly across the paper, allowing the ridges and folds in the cardstock to pick up the ink. Trim edges of cardstock and adhere to page background. Line edges of green cardstock with thin strips of black cardstock and brads.

Amy Farnsworth, Sandy, Utah

Supplies: *Round letter stickers (Doodlebug Design); letter die cuts (QuicKutz); black stamping ink (Stewart Superior); gingham ribbon (Offray); black, charcoal, slate and green cardstocks; square brads; paint chip*

Snapshots of One

COORDINATE INK WITH PATTERNED PAPER

Summer created several handmade page elements to match her inked page background. Choose an ink color that matches patterned papers. Ink edges of cream cardstock background with burgundy. Tear script paper and brush burgundy ink around edges. Cut out tags using template and tear cream cardstock for photo mats. Add ink to all edges of photo mats and tags.

Summer Ford, San Antonio, Texas

Supplies: *Patterned papers (Anna Griffin, 7 Gypsies); curved letter stamps (EK Success); small capital letter stamps (Hero Arts); Baroque Burgundy stamping ink (Stampin' Up!); date stamp (Making Memories); buttons (Blumenthal Lansing); tag template (Provo Craft); red and white fibers (Fibers By The Yard); cream and burgundy cardstocks; embroidery floss*

TIP: Applying clear ink and extra thick embossing powder over already-inked flower stamps can give them a freshly watered look.

Springtime

DECORATE A TITLE'S BACKGROUND

To echo the light and airy feel of a spring day spent in Boulder, Colorado, Holle used tulip stamps behind her title letters. First, rub edges of blue background and red photo mats with white ink. For title background, stamp tulips in green and red inks, then stamp over each with watermark ink. Apply extra thick embossing powder and heat. Stamp title letters in black over tulips.

Holle Wiktorek, Reunion, Colorado
Photos: Georgia Norman, Nashville, Tennessee

Supplies: *Tulip stamp, white stamping ink and Rose Red, Basic Black, Garden Green and Ballet Blue stamping inks (Stampin' Up!); VersaMark watermark ink (Tsukineko); Grace letter stamps (La Pluma); Button letter stamps (PSX Design); clear Ultra Thick Embossing Enamel powder (Ranger); fibers (Lion Brand); black, red and blue cardstocks; silver brad; foam tape; white pen; memorabilia*

Book of Me

UNIFY A MINI ALBUM WITH STAMPED COLLAGES

Using various stamps and colors across page backgrounds, Corinne created a 6 x 6" album about her youth. Use black ink to stamp images on page backgrounds. After stamping, color backgrounds using various bright colored ink pads. Overlap some colors for a continuous, blended look.

Corinne Cullen Hawkins, Walnut Creek, California

Supplies: *Lizard stamp (Mostly Animals), parasol girl stamp (Stamp Oasis), Godzilla stamp (JudiKins), beret girl stamp (source unknown); circuit board stamp (Above the Mark), open widow stamp (Art Impressions); Gypsy dancer stamp (Fruit Basket Upset); Aztec butterfly, leaping dancer, "Mama said...", beach friends and girl on beach stamps (Stampin' Up!); Paintbox rainbow stamping inks (Clearsnap); letter stickers (source unknown), clear page pebble (Creative Imaginations); white, cream, tan, yellow, blue and green cardstocks; white embossing powder; deckle scissors; white tags; gold brads; gold twine; black pen*

Quacky Favors

USE A BRAYER FOR
A UNIQUE BACKGROUND

Heidi created a colorful grid pattern as a backdrop for a playful page featuring Easter crafts. Apply strips of low-tack masking tape around all edges of cream cardstock, crossing at the corners. Completely cover a brayer with ink from a multi-colored pad by rolling it in the same direction across the pad each time. Roll the brayer over the tape grid, again pressing the brayer in the same direction. Apply several layers of ink until desired color is achieved; let dry. Peel off tape to reveal stripes.

Heidi Schueller, Waukesha, Wisconsin

Supplies: *Colorbox multicolored stamping ink (Clearsnap); low-tack tape (Stamp It!); fibers (Timeless Touches); embossing paste (Dreamweaver Stencils); clear embossing powder (Ranger); letter stickers (Mrs. Grossman's); circle clip (Target); white, yellow, orange and rust cardstocks; rubber brayer; buttons; feathers; chalks; foam tape*

TIP: When finding the right patterned paper background to match photos is difficult, brayering ink over masking tape is a good technique to try. Multicolored ink pads are the perfect supply to use with a brayer when more than one shade is desired.

Dear Mom

ENHANCE A DESIGN
WITH PIGMENT POWDERS

Using a background stamp with a recessed image, Nicole created metallic mats for her photos. Stamp leaf pattern on cardstock with watermark ink. Brush on metallic pigment powders with a small, soft paintbrush. Trim cardstocks to mat photos and title letters.

Nicole LaCour, Memory Makers magazine

Supplies: *Patterned papers (Magenta); Holle's Inspiration letter and Rose Leaf background stamps (Prickley Pear Rubber Stamps); VersaMark watermark ink (Tsukineko); Perfect Pearls Bronze, Rust, Copper and Sunflower Sparkle metallic pigment powders (Ranger); metal label holder (Li'l Davis Designs); vellum; eyelets; pale mauve cardstock*

Looking *at* You

I swear yesterday you grew a foot taller. I'm not sure how it happened, but I know that *the last time I looked at you,* you definitely weren't able to look me square in the eye. When exactly did you get to the point where, when you want me to brush your hair, you have to sit on the floor? I know that the last time I looked at you, I could fix it just standing next to you in the bathroom.

Who gave you permission to go and grow up on me? I certainly don't remember doing that. As a matter of fact, I know that I distinctly told you that I always wanted you to stay little. Either you just didn't listen to me, or, more likely the case, you can't help it. You're growing up despite my best efforts. *The last time I looked at you,* though, I know I saw a little girl. But this morning, I saw you with fresh eyes. I caught more than a glimpse of the young woman you're becoming — and it's an amazing and wonderful thing. Enjoy it.

March 4, 2004

Looking at You

CREATE PATTERNED PAPER
WITH SHADOW STAMPS

Using a collection of square and rectangle stamps, Becky designed her own patterned background paper. Decide on a pattern in which to arrange the stamps and apply to white cardstock using pink, rose and beige inks. For variety, slightly modify the pattern for the second page.

Becky Thompson, Fruitland, Idaho

Supplies: *Rectangle background, Wavy Background, Fuzzy Edge Background, Little Greetings Background, Three Solids Background stamps and Wheat Shadow stamping ink (Hero Arts); ¾" square stamp (Limited Edition Rubber Stamps); Seashell Pink stamping ink (Ranger); Soft Rose stamping ink (Stewart Superior); metal and rub-on letters (Making Memories); metal tag (Manto Fev); metal charms (Jo-Ann Fabrics); square punch (Marvy); pink and white cardstocks; vellum; black pen; brads*

TIP: Before covering an entire background with shadow stamps, practice stamping them in different patterns on scrap paper. When you are pleased with an arrangement, duplicate it for your background. In addition, try overlapping stamps to achieve unique colors and patterns.

Thank You

COVER A BRAYER WITH PLASTIC WRAP

To create an interesting texture on her card's background, Tara stamped a vineyard image and added a shimmering effect with a brayer.

Tara Bazota, Thornton, Colorado

Supplies: *Vineyard background stamp, Etruscan stamp, Eggplant Envy stamping ink and Glassy Glaze embossing powder (Stampin' Up!); acrylic brayer (Speedball); Gold Encore Metallic ink (Tsukineko); black, gold and purple cardstocks; black fibers, oval eyelets, plastic wrap*

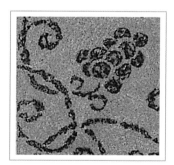

STEP-BY-STEP: BRAYERED PLASTIC WRAP TECHNIQUE

1 Stamp design with eggplant ink on eggplant cardstock. Sprinkle with clear powder and heat emboss.

2 Cover brayer's roller with a piece of clear plastic wrap. Apply gold ink to brayer and roll over embossed pattern for a crinkled effect.

3 Use a tissue to wipe gold ink away from embossed designs. Repeat the same process for stamped image at center of card.

Correspondence
SPONGE BACKGROUND COLOR

Tracy created a soft color treatment by sponging ink onto her card. Trim piece of tan cardstock and stamp script pattern in green ink. Stamp center image in black, trim, mat with green cardstock and adhere to card. Using a small makeup sponge lightly dabbed in green ink, tap ink over background and center image. Tear bottom and apply ink to edge.

Tracy Burtt, Lake Kiowa, Texas

Supplies: *French Script and Letters for Friends stamps; Old Olive and Basic Black stamping inks and sheer ribbon (Stampin' Up!); green, olive and white cardstocks; makeup sponge*

Warmest Wishes
STAMP A MULTICOLORED BACKGROUND

Using a square decorative stamp, Tara created a lively stair-step background. Ink stamp with rust-colored ink and impress the image on cardstock. Clean the stamp, load it with yellow ink and stamp directly above the rust image. Stamp the same image above the yellow one with green ink. Repeat until three short, straight columns are completed. Turn stamped columns on a slight angle and trim to fit front of card. Trimming at an angle produces the stair-step effect.

Tara Bazata, Thornton, Colorado
Original Design: Trish Griggs

Supplies: *Elegant Ornaments and Year Round Cheer I stamp sets, More Mustard, Really Rust and Old Olive stamping inks (Stampin' Up!); mustard, rust, olive and cream cardstocks; sheer gold ribbon; gold twine; eyelet*

Vintage Christmas
BRAYER A TRANSPARENT BACKGROUND

Erikia achieved a vintage look by painting a transparency with a brayer. Cover a brayer with copper acrylic paint and gently roll onto the back of a transparency. Repeat the process with magenta paint. Use black solvent ink to stamp images onto the front of the transparency. Add a premade vintage image in the center and surround with gold glitter.

Erikia Ghumm, Brighton, Colorado

Supplies: *Blank greeting card (DMD); Script patterned paper (K & Company); mail stamp (Inkadinkado); StazOn black solvent ink (Tsukineko); star nailheads (JewelCraft); vintage photograph (Artchix Studio); transparency; copper and magenta acrylic paints; glitter glue; craft knife, brayer*

PRACTICE HARD

practice (prak´.tis) 1. to engage in a specific activity frequently as to become proficient 2. to act as to perfect

teamwork (tem´.wurk) 1. joint action by a group of people

commitment (ke.mit´.mint) 1. to dedicate oneself to something or someone 2. duty; promise

sportsmanship (sports´.man.ship) 1.one who plays fair; can lose without complaint or win without gloating

teammate (tem´.mat) 1. an individual on the same team, with unique abilities, working toward the same goal

success (sek.ses´) 1. a favorable result 2. gaining of wealth, fame or recognition 3. attaining one's aspirations

PLAY HARDER

MARKIE

YOUTH YOUTH YOUTH YOUTH YOUTH YOUTH YOUTH
It is a happy talent to know how to play *youth* -Ralph Waldo Emerson
Through our good fortune, in our youth our hearts are touched with fire. It was given to us to learn at the outset that life is a proufound and passionate thing. -Oliver Wendell Holmes

Chapter 3
Lettering and Titles

Stamped pages receive a voice of their own when you add bold titles and dainty journaling with letter stamps. Find silhouetted stamped titles, stamping on ribbon, embossed words, bulleted journaling and stamping on wood chips in this chapter, just to name a few. Learn even more about stamped lettering and titles by following step-by-step instructions for:

Supplies: *Patterned paper (Li'l Davis Designs); foam letter stamps (Making Memories); pink acrylic paint (Plaid); ballet stickers (Deluxe Designs); transparency; black, pink and white cardstocks; brads*

Dancing Queen

STAMP TITLE WITH ACRYLIC PAINT

Kathryn used foam letter stamps and acrylic paint to create a bold title that stands out on a black background.

Kathryn Allen, Hamilton, Ohio

STEP-BY-STEP: STAMPING WITH ACRYLIC PAINT

1 Trim and layer patterned paper on black cardstock background. With a ruler and a pencil, draw guidelines on black cardstock for title words.

2 Squirt acrylic paint on paper plate. Press foam letter stamps into paint. Dab excess paint on the paper plate several times, then press letters onto cardstock using pencil lines as a guide.

Introducing
Isabella Alexis

STAMP TITLE ON VELLUM

On a strip of pink vellum, Janetta embossed her title letters. Apply black ink to letters and stamp first word of title. Sprinkle clear embossing powder, tap off excess and heat until the image appears glossy and raised. With one word finished, stamp next word and emboss, then proceed to the last word.

Janetta Abucejo Wieneke, Memory Makers Books
Photos: Jonathan Abucejo, Copley, Ohio

Supplies: *Patterned papers (Scrapworks); Bradbury letter stamps (Plaid); Holle's Inspiration letter stamps (Prickley Pear Rubber Stamps); VersaFine Onyx Black stamping ink VersaMark watermark ink (Tsukineko); clear embossing powder and silver embossing pearls (Ranger); date stamp (Magnetic Poetry); round number stamps (PSX Design); paper flower and ribbon (Me & My Big Ideas); lime green and pale pink cardstocks; pink vellum; black slide mount*

TIP: When stamping and embossing a title with lots of words or letters, emboss one word before proceeding to the next so the ink does not start to dry.

Play Time

STAMP TITLE LETTERS ON BLOCKS OF COLORED PAPER

Michelle made the second word in her title interesting by stamping letters on small colored blocks of paper. Stamp one letter each in black ink on pink, purple, green and blue papers. Trim into small blocks and mat on black cardstock. In addition, stamp the date of the event on another block and frame it with a painted label holder.

Michelle Keeth, Lowell, Arkansas

Supplies: *Striped and solid papers (SEI); letter stamps (Hero Arts); photo holders, label holder, black paint and date stamps (Making Memories); transparency (Artistic Expressions); Brilliance black stamping ink (Tsukineko); black and white cardstocks; eyelets; black pen*

My Chili Head

DECORATE WOVEN PAPER

To document her son's love for hot and spicy foods, Pam stamped her title and chili pepper embellishment on woven specialty paper that resembles a placemat. Load large foam letters with red and green acrylic paints and press them onto specialty paper. Stamp chili pepper on specialty paper, cut out and adhere next to title.

Pam Canavan, Clermont, Florida

Supplies: *Woven specialty paper (Be Unique); red/yellow patterned paper (KI Memories); foam letter stamps, acrylic paints and black rub-ons (Making Memories); pepper stamp (Close To My Heart); VersaMark watermark ink (Tsukineko); transparency (3M); paper yarn*

Walk in the Pines

STAMP ON TWILL TAPE

Gwen created her own twill word strip by stamping letters onto a twill ribbon. Use an acrylic block and double-sided adhesive to hold unmounted stamps spelling the word "walk." Stamp the word several times in brown ink along tan twill tape. After cutting the tape into two sections, adhere the long strip at the top of the page and a single word near the main title. Stamp the rest of the title in brown directly on page background.

Gwen Dye, Enterprise, Alabama

Supplies: *Patterned paper (Mustard Moon); "walk" letter stamps (found at dollar store); Neuland letter stamps (Wordsworth); Sepia archival stamping ink (Ranger); button embellishments (EK Success); brown and cream cardstocks; twill tape; brown pen*

Panda Bears

COMBINE SETS OF LETTER STAMPS ON A PAGE

Beverly used four letter stamp sets to create the words on this page. Stamp large foam letters with red acrylic paint for a title on patterned paper. Use a small set for stamping metal-rimmed tags. Outline the small stamped words with black pen. For the remaining words, combine two stamp fonts by using one for the initial letters and another for the rest of the words.

Beverly Sizemore, Sulligent, Alabama

Supplies: *Patterned paper (KI Memories); foam letter stamps (Making Memories); panda stamp set (Stampin' Up!); Cardinal red acrylic paint (Plaid); Ancient Page black stamping ink (Clearsnap); Button letter stamps (PSX Design); letter stamps (Stampabilities); Jive letter stamps and clear embossing powder (All Night Media); red fibers (EK Success); circle punches (Family Treasures); black, white and red cardstocks, silver eyelets*

Fall Festival

STAMP ON RIBBONS

Beverly used dark orange ink to stamp her title, names and date onto grosgrain ribbon. Tape the ends of the ribbon to your work surface to prevent it from shifting. Stamp letters onto ribbon. Accent ribbons with ribbon charms and adhere to page.

Beverly Sizemore, Sulligent, Alabama

Supplies: *Patterned paper and leaf punch (EK Success); orange ribbon (WFR Ribbon Corporation); letter stamps (All Night Media); Ancient Page Sienna stamping ink (Clearsnap); Only Orange stamping ink (Stampin' Up!); metal ribbon charms (Making Memories); gold and rust cardstocks; chalk; foam tape*

TIP: Before stamping on ribbon, test the ink on a scrap piece of ribbon of the same type to see how visible the ink color will be when it dries.

In Bloom

SILHOUETTE TITLE LETTERS

Saralyn designed a title that really pops against her background and successfully balances her eye-catching flower photograph. Stamp title letters with red acrylic paint on white cardstock. Using a craft knife, cut out letters, leaving a rim of white cardstock around each one. Mount letters with foam tape on green computer-printed cardstock.

Saralyn Berkowitz, Long Beach, New York

Supplies: *Patterned paper (Chatterbox); Jersey foam letter stamps, red acrylic paint, Heidi rub-on letters and metal-rimmed tag (Making Memories); tulip charm (source unknown); black, white, green and red cardstocks; twine; foam tape*

Killing Time

MIX TYPE STYLES FOR PHOTO CAPTIONS

Katie combined three font sets to create her title and photo captions. Stamp letters on scrap paper to find a pleasing composition. Re-create placement by stamping directly on page background with brown ink. Tear top edge of cream cardstock, ink edges and adhere to page. Add more words to cream cardstock. For title, stamp letters on rust cardstock and cut apart into small rectangles. Ink edges of each title letter and adhere to green strip through center of cream cardstock.

Katie Swanson, South Milwaukee, Wisconsin

Supplies: *Rust patterned paper (Cock-A-Doodle Design); Polaroid and It's My type unmounted letter stamps (Ma Vinci's); letter stamps (Stampin' Up!); Vivid Coffee Bean stamping ink (Clearsnap); brown stamping ink (Ranger); light and dark green and cream cardstocks; brads*

Abundance of Abundance

HIGHLIGHT LETTERS WITH GOLD PAINT

Lisa recorded the many seasonal blessings she experienced, despite not having snow for the holidays. Ink foam letter stamps with a sponge brush using red and green paints; let dry. Using gold paint and a thin paintbrush, highlight the right side of each letter. Embellish other parts of the page with splatters of gold paint to coordinate.

Lisa Jobson, Ajax, Ontario, Canada

Supplies: Patterned papers (Karen Foster Design, 7 Gypsies); Philadelphia foam letter stamps, Cranberry and Evergreen paints, fabric sayings and colored staples (Making Memories); Rich Gold paint (Jo Sonja's); wire reindeer embellishment (Westrim); gold photo corners (Boutique Trims); mini frame (Card Connection); tinker pin (7 Gypsies); red, green and taupe cardstocks; fabric; green ribbon; black rickrack; beads

TIP: Foam stamps tend to slide if heavily loaded with paint. To avoid this, watch how much paint you are applying to the stamp and be careful not to press too hard onto the paper.

2 Times the Trouble

STAMP TITLE LETTERS ON TOP OF PHOTOS AND MATS

A rough-and-tumble boy page called for a large, bold stamped title. Tear and layer several patterned papers for page background. Mat photo and layer on background. Apply black paint to foam letter stamps. Stamp title words across background, allowing them to overlap the photo mat and photo. Tear the word "trouble" from a piece of patterned paper and mount in bottom right corner to finish title. Add metal accents to support the design.

Stacie Gammill, Sulphur Springs, Texas

Supplies: Patterned papers (Carolee's Creations, Paper Loft, Sweetwater, 7 Gypsies); Jersey foam letter stamps, aluminum mesh and fabric label (Making Memories); metal photo corners and chain (Karen Foster Design); date stamp (Wal-Mart); metal letter conchos (Clearsnap); brads; nailheads; black paint; sandpaper

Glimpse

CUT OUT LETTERS STAMPED WITH WATERMARK INK

By using watermark ink only with letter stamps, Kah-Mei allowed the pattern on her paper to shine through. Stamp letters with watermark ink onto patterned paper. Although no ink color can be seen, the ink will deepen the color of the paper. Following the outline of the ink, cut out letters. Adhere them to patterned background with foam tape.

Kah-Mei Smith, Coquitlam, British Columbia, Canada

Supplies: *Patterned papers (Creative Imaginations, 7 Gypsies, Wordsworth); patterned vellum (American Crafts); word stickers (Creative Imaginations); It's My Type letter stamps (Ma Vinci's); VersaMark watermark ink (Tsukineko); daisy die cuts (Paper House Productions); slide mounts (KI Memories); metal frame (Scrapworks); label maker stickers (Pebbles); mini album (Kolo); circle punch; fibers; ribbons; brads; eyelets; jewelry tags; large tag; small washers; chalk; black pen; foam tape*

Ben

STAMP A BRIGHT TITLE ON A DARK BACKGROUND

Sam's title brings out the color of the plastic Easter eggs in her photos. Using bright green acrylic paint, stamp foam letters onto black patterned background paper. Add clear letter stickers over each stamped letter. Color edges of background, one photo and page accent with green paint to coordinate.

Sam Cousins, Trumbull, Connecticut

Supplies: *Patterned paper (Sweetwater); white card with holes (DMD); rub-on words (Royal & Langnickel); green, orange, purple, blue and pink acrylic paints and silver photo corners (Making Memories); felt egg coaster (Target); letter stickers (Maya Road); eyelash fibers (Fibers By The Yard); ribbon; black pen*

Working Together

ALTERNATE LETTER STAMPS

Stacy's title saves space while adding an interesting design element. Cut a 10½ x 2" strip of tan cardstock. Measure and mark the center point of strip. Stamp the "k" at the center point with dark pink ink. Stamp letters for "together" outward from the center "k" in blue ink, spreading them evenly to fill the space. Stamp the rest of the smaller letters in between the larger ones. Shade strip with brown ink. Mat with cork sheet and attach photo holders as accents.

Stacy Yoder, Yucaipa, California

Supplies: *Patterned papers (Chatterbox); Reliquary letter stamps (Ma Vinci's); uppercase letter stamps and dark pink stamping ink (PSX Design); Night of Navy and Close to Cocoa stamping inks (Stampin' Up!); fabric mesh (Magenta); photo holders (7 Gypsies); black and tan cardstocks; crocheted lace; cork sheet; eyelets; brads; sewing machine*

Night and Day

STAMP AND EMBOSS TITLE ON TEXTURED PAPER

Cindy used reverse-image unmounted letter stamps to achieve her title's unique look. Ink stamps sparingly with black ink and press lightly onto white textured cardstock. When applied lightly, texture should show through ink. Repeat with orange ink for second word. Cut out each letter, leaving a thin frame of white around each one. Emboss the letters with extra-fine embossing powder.

Cindy Jarrett, Chesapeake, Virginia

Supplies: *Patterned papers (All My Memories, Chatterbox, KI Memories, Rusty Pickle); Reliquary Type Negative letter stamps (Ma Vinci's); square letter brads and "&" charm (Colorbök); Colorbox black and orange stamping inks (Clearsnap); clear embossing powder (Ranger); label maker (Dymo); orange, black and white cardstocks; ribbons; fabric; eyelets; yellow snaps*

Wet

EMBOSS WITH TWO COLORS OF POWDER

To create a title feature that appears wet, Lisa layered two colors of embossing powders. Stamp the letters in clear embossing ink and sprinkle with teal embossing powder. Heat set. Add another layer of embossing ink and emboss with copper embossing powder. To bring out the shine of the letters and further communicate the wet theme, dab on clear paper glaze.

Lisa Francis, New Castle, Indiana

Supplies: *Gold letters (Office Max); ribbons and page pebbles (Making Memories); Macquarie (teal) and Sunburnt (terra cotta bronze) Opals embossing powders (Pipe Dreamink); letter stamps (Ma Vinci's); green cardstock; tan tag; library pocket; beaded fringe; microscope slide; walnut ink; paper glaze; brown pen*

TIP: Apply colored ink over stamped images after embossing them to achieve a resist or reverse-image look. The ink will not stick to the embossed areas.

Flamingos

SUBSTITUTE AN IMAGE STAMP FOR A LETTER

To form the letter "I" in her title, Jodi added a large flamingo stamp that she embossed and silhouetted. For title, cut letters from cardstock using computer fonts as guides. Apply clear ink to the letters and sprinkle on several different colored embossing powders. Heat letters for a multi-toned look. Heat copper embossing powder around edges of the stencil letter "F." For coordinating border strips, apply clear ink to a roller stamp and roll images along cardstock strips. Emboss strips and dab chalk stamping inks along the strips. Repeat process for single flamingo images. Emboss edges of strips and coordinating buttons with copper embossing powder.

Jodi Amidei, Memory Makers Books

Supplies: *Large flamingo stamp (Inkadinkado); flamingo roller stamp (Stampin' Up); pink and peach Colorbox chalk stamping inks (Clearsnap); VersaMark clear stamping ink (Tsukineko); colored embossing powders (Stamp A Mania, Stampendous!, Tsukineko); textured rust cardstock (Bazzill); buttons (Blumenthal Lansing); eyelets (Creative Imaginations); twill ribbon (Scenic Route Paper Co.); patterned fabric; transparency; acrylic paint*

We Must Teach

CHOOSE STAMPS TO ECHO A PAGE THEME

To enhance the youthful feel of teaching children to read, Lilia stamped letters resembling alphabet blocks for her title. Use a ruler and pencil to draw baselines for stamps. Stamp letters on cream cardstock in black ink. Tilt letters on the baseline for a whimsical look. Stamp design in black next to title.

Lilia Meredith, Scottsdale, Arizona

Supplies: *Patterned papers (Rusty Pickle, SEI); block letter stamps (Hero Arts); swirl stamp (Making Memories); leaf stamp (Inkadinkado); StazOn black solvent ink (Tsukineko); Antique Linen distress ink (Ranger); vintage cut-out (Hot Off The Press); mini frame charm (7 Gypsies); square punch (Marvy); black ribbon (Darice); purple fibers; lavender and cream cardstocks; black grosgrain ribbon; black rickrack*

Kaleb

MIX LETTER SIZES FOR EMPHASIS

By using three sizes of letter stamps, Rachael emphasized different words on her page. Cut strips of 11 x 3" and 11 x 5¼" patterned paper. On thinner strip, stamp boy's name in black acrylic paint using uppercase foam letter stamps. Add corner stamp. On wider strip, stamp "time" in lowercase letters with black paint, followed by corner stamp. Fill in space around "time" by adding smaller stamped words.

Rachael Giallongo, Auburn, New Hampshire

Supplies: *Patterned paper (KI Memories); large foam letter stamps, corner stamp and black paint (Making Memories); small letter stamps (PSX Design); patterned transparency (K & Company); label maker (Dymo); turquoise and olive cardstocks*

Grow

STAMP ON WOOD CHIPS

For a circle journal on the topic "What Brings You Joy," Kah-Mei chose gardening. She added wood-chip letters as an organic element to support the theme. Apply paint to wood chips with finger until surface is covered; let paint dry. Use brown ink to stamp one letter on each chip. Cover surface with thick, clear gloss and allow to dry. Attach wood-chip letters to accordion-folded cardstock and journal in between the chips. Fold journaling and tuck behind paper strips secured with brads. Place another wood-chip letter on the front of accordian-folded element. For title, stamp letter outlines in brown ink on patterned paper. Cut letters apart into rectangles and double mat with brown and gold cardstocks.

Kah-Mei Smith, Coquitlam, British Columbia, Canada

Supplies: *Patterned papers (Anna Griffin, Chatterbox, Deluxe Designs, Provo Craft); flower bunch and tree outline stamps (source unknown); outlined letter stamps and capital letter stamps (FontWerks); lowercase letter stamps and circle letter stamps (PSX Design); brown stamping ink (Ranger); "homegrown" sticker (Pebbles); Triple thick clear gloss (DecoArt); gold, green and brown cardstocks; wood chips; brads; black mesh; jute; black, red and metallic colored pens; sewing machine*

Marching Bravely Toward the Unknown

STAMP TITLE VERTICALLY

Cheryl brought emphasis to her page by stamping her title alongside her focal-point photo. With a ruler and pencil, draw a vertical guideline on patterned paper background. Use brown ink to stamp large lowercase title letters along the line. Write small title words next to stamped word with brown pen. Balance the title by adding horizontal elements: a strip of patterned ABC paper, a tape measure, twine and watch label holder.

Cheryl Manz, Paulding, Ohio

Supplies: *Patterned papers (Scenic Route Paper Co., 7 Gypsies); letter stamps (River City Rubber Works); StazOn Timber Brown solvent ink (Tsukineko); letter stickers (Me & My Big Ideas); leaf charms (Scrapworks); watch label holder, key charm and wooden letter tiles (EK Success); "together" word (Li'l Davis Designs); tan cardstock; twine; tape measure; brown pen*

Shine Like the Sun

FORM A DESIGN ELEMENT WITH LETTER STAMPS

With two shades of gold cardstock, Katie created a small color-blocked design that includes her title. Cut small blocks of light and dark gold cardstocks. Ink edges of all blocks and arrange together. Punch sun shapes from gold, ink edges and adhere to bottom three cardstock rectangles. With the smallest set, stamp thematic words on certain blocks in brown ink. Allow certain words to slightly overlap sun punches. Stamp additional small words on other pieces of gold cardstock, cut around words, ink edges and adhere to other blocks. For title, stamp two type styles next to one another on dark gold. On lighter gold from a third type style, stamp the word "sun" and punch out with circle punch. Ink edges of circles and adhere with other title words. Cut out title in a rectangle, ink edges and attach to largest block with foam tape. Wrap embroidery floss around edges of title for emphasis.

Katie Swanson, South Milwaukee, Wisconsin

Supplies: *Olive patterned paper (source unknown); Funky letter stamps (Wordsworth); small letter stamps and metal charms (Making Memories); Love Letters stamps (PSX Design); brown stamping ink (Ranger); Vivid Coffee Bean stamping ink (Clearsnap); sun, leaf, flower and circle punches (EK Success); light and dark gold cardstocks; brads; brown embroidery floss; foam tape*

There it is again. That look. The one you get when you are deep in thought trying to figure out the meaning of life or just trying to figure out what to get into next. I love it when you have that look. I know then that you are really growing up and learning to apply deep thought to situations. I hope that your deep thinking will continue as you mature and grow into manhood. If it does you will always be able to think through situations rather than just react. What a virtue this will be.

Consider him who endured such opposition from sinful men, so that you will not grow weary and lose heart. Hebrews 12:3

Supplies: *Script patterned paper (K & Company); Classic letter stamps and inks (All Night Media); Apple Barrel Caramel Candy paint (Plaid); metallic rub-ons (Craf-T); air-dry clay (Hearty); brown cardstock*

Boyhood

STAMP INTO AIR-DRY CLAY

For a rugged look that matched her page theme and color scheme, Renee created her title by stamping into clay.

Renee Hagler, Birmingham, Alabama

STEP-BY-STEP: CLAY TITLE LETTERS

1 Roll balls of clay about the size of marbles for each letter in title. Flatten balls into discs and stamp letters in centers with black ink.

2 Paint each disc with brown acrylic paint. When the clay dries, re-stamp letters in black ink.

3 Apply metallic rub-ons with your finger tip around edges of each letter.

Adorable You

JOURNAL WITH LETTER STAMPS

In place of journaling, Brandi stamped brief descriptions of her daughter's features onto strips of cardstock. With small letters, stamp words on brown cardstock with dark brown ink. Cut out words into thin rectangles and ink edges with black. Attach to page with brads. Choose letter stickers for the title that coordinate with journaling strips.

Brandi Barnes, Kelso, Tennessee

Supplies: *Patterned paper (Carolee's Creations); Rummage magnetic letter stamps (Making Memories); brown and black stamping inks (Rubber Stampede); letter stickers (K & Company); brown, sage and cream cardstocks; brads*

Thanksgiving Through Mischon's Eyes

CREATE PHOTO CAPTIONS WITH CLAY

To highlight the photos taken by her four-year-old daughter, Nancy created "stone" name tags for each family member. Roll clay into balls and flatten into irregular ovals. Press letter stamps inked with black into clay. To add texture, gently press a stencil paintbrush into the clay's surface. After clay is dry, shade the edges with tan paint.

Nancy Stinemetz, Danville, Indiana

Supplies: *Leaf patterned paper (Provo Craft); leaf stickers and fibers (EK Success); air-dry clay (Creative Paperclay); Stenography magnetic letter stamps (Making Memories); Colorbox Gold, Black and Ancient Page Chocolate Brown inks (Clearsnap); Country Tan paint (Plaid); evergreen and gold cardstocks; vellum; eyelets*

NYC

STAMP A SIMPLE CONTRASTING TITLE

On this title page of her New York City vacation album, Amanda highlighted her favorite images and left enough space for a simple stamped title. Arrange photos on background, leaving space for title. Stamp title on black cardstock with 2½" foam letter stamps lightly covered with white acrylic paint.

Amanda Goodwin, Munroe Falls, Ohio

Supplies: *Foam letter stamps, word washer and ribbon (Making Memories); white acrylic paint (Plaid); label maker (Dymo); black and white cardstocks; staples*

This Is Me

JOURNAL OVER A STAMPED TITLE

Laura melds her title and journaling together on this page. Using green, blue and gold inks, stamp title words on block of tan cardstock. When ink dries, journal over title with black pen. Repeat this method inside the tag book: Stamp the word "me" on each page and write journaling over the stamped words.

Laura Kurz, Gambrills, Maryland

Supplies: *Print block patterned paper (Pebbles); It's My Type letter stamps (Ma Vinci's); typewriter key stamps (EK Success); small letter stamps (PSX Design); Mediterranean stamping inks (Clearsnap); tags (7 Gypsies); taupe, brown and tan cardstocks; black pen; snap; sewing machine*

TIP: If you wish to stamp lettering on distressed paper, complete all your stamping and let it dry before distressing. Crumpling the paper beforehand will make lining up words and letters more difficult.

Why I Love America

MIX UPPER- AND LOWER-CASE LETTERS

Michelle says she likes to be spontaneous about her lettering to create a comfortable, homey feel on her layouts. Brainstorm a list of words that describe love for one's country. Using blue ink, stamp words on tan cardstock using a mixture of upper- and lowercase letters. Cut cardstock into strips and shapes, crumple them and flatten out. Brush crumpled pieces with brown ink. For an interesting effect around a photo, apply white paint to the end of corrugated cardboard and stamp a frame.

Michelle Keeth, Lowell, Arkansas

Supplies: *Patterned paper (Karen Foster Design); star stamps (Wal-Mart); white acrylic paint (Delta); Pastel Pop and Classic letter stamps (Hero Arts); Antique uppercase and lowercase letter stamps (PSX Design); Brilliance blue stamping ink (Clearsnap); Nick Bantock VanDyke Brown stamping ink (Ranger); star eyelets and plaque, metal letter charms and metal-rimmed tags (Making Memories); star eyelets; navy, blue, tan and white cardstocks; silver brads; black and red pens*

Supplies: *Square patterned and solid vellums, circle punches, vellum bubble embellishments, navy epoxy tiles and circular corner punch (EK Success); Chunky letter stamps (Stampendous!); Playful number stamps (Hero Arts); Antique uppercase, lowercase and Piccadilly letter stamps (PSX Design); VersaMark watermark ink (Tsukineko); white embossing powder (Ranger); blue, white and olive cardstocks; turquoise vellum; white and black pens*

TIP: So that some of the excess embossing powder will remain around the stamped letters as seen here, do not rub tiles or vellum with an anti-static pouch before stamping. So that even more powder will stick around the stamped words, sprinkle on more powder and reheat the surface immediately after embossing the words.

Bubbles

EMBOSS ON EPOXY SQUARES AND VELLUM

With bubbles floating in her photos, Michelle created a page filled with them. For smaller words and date, use watermark ink and letter stamps to stamp on epoxy tiles. Sprinkle a liberal amount of white embossing powder on the tiles and gently tap off some of the excess. Heat tiles. For title and boy's name, stamp letters onto vellum with watermark ink again, add powder, shake off some and emboss again. Punch letters and word from vellum using a circle punch. Stamp and emboss other words around the spread.

Michelle Keeth, Lowell, Arkansas

Being a Man

HIGHLIGHT THE FIRST LETTERS OF TITLE WORDS IN A RUGGED FONT

The letters "B," "A" and "M" in Megan's title add interest to her title since they were stamped in a rugged style. Adhere unmounted letter stamps to an acrylic block using double-sided adhesive. Use one font set to stamp the first letters of each title word on striped paper with brown ink. Use a second letter stamp set for the rest of the title. Ink edges of top of journaling blocks to coordinate with title style.

Megan Friesen, Chilliwack, British Columbia, Canada

Supplies: *Patterned papers (Chatterbox, Making Memories, 7 Gypsies); decorative brad (Making Memories); Base 02 Upper and Hopeless Heart Lower letter stamps (FontWerks); Nick Bantock Van Dyke Brown stamping ink (Ranger); picture hanger charm (Jest Charming); brown and tan cardstocks; ribbon; twill tape; brads*

Snow

ENHANCE A THEME WITH STAMPED LETTERS

Joy's choice of letter stamps for the word "snow" enhances her winter theme. Choose a letter stamp style that gives a cold feeling and seems to spill ice crystals onto the page. With black ink, stamp letters on white textured cardstock. Pair the title with a computer font that has a similar effect. Round out a chilly design by using black-and-white photos and embellishments. Trim edes of page and mount on a red background for a bit of color.

Joy Bohon, Bedford, Indiana

Supplies: *Patterned paper (KI Memories); Base 02 letter stamps (Font-Werks); Memories black stamping ink (Stewart Superior); bottle cap and puzzle letters (Li'l Davis Designs); photo holder (7 Gypsies); film strip (Creative Imaginations); label maker (Dymo); white textured cardstock (Bazzill); black and red cardstocks; black brad*

TIP: If you want to emboss computer fonts, print from an inkjet printer—the process won't work on laser print-outs. To emboss fonts that are extremely delicate or small, use extra-fine embossing powder for the best readability.

October Memories

EMBOSS A COMPUTER-PRINTED TITLE

Angelia chose two computer fonts for her title, then gave them a stamped effect by heat embossing. Immediately after printing text on vellum so that ink is still warm and moist, sprinkle black embossing powder on the words. Gently blow off any stray bits of powder and heat with an embossing gun to create a glossy finish.

Angelia Wiggington, Belmont, Mississippi

Supplies: *Patterned papers and butterfly stickers (K & Company); black embossing powder (Ranger); metal hinge (Magic Scraps); black photo corners (Canson); vellum; lavender cardstock; blue sheer ribbon; foam tape*

Tree Hunting Foray

COMBINE WATERMARK AND COLORED INKS

Michaela stamped meaningful words with watermark and chalk inks for both her title and a background design. On tan cardstock, stamp two title words with watermark ink to deepen the color of the paper, leaving space in between the two words. With black ink, stamp second word in title between the two watermarked words. Trim edges of green cardstock and stamp large words across it in several different ink colors. Finish by stamping a few small words in black ink. Note: The right side of the spread folds out multiple times, first to reveal journaling and then to reveal additional photos, as shown in the inset shots.

Michaela Young-Mitchell, Morenci, Arizona

Supplies: *Stencil letter stamps (Ma Vinci's); Antique letter stamps and black stamping ink (PSX Design); VersaMark watermark ink (Tsukineko); Colorbox Chestnut Roan, Alabaster, Bisque and Lime Pastel fluid chalk stamping inks (Clearsnap); gingham ribbon (Offray); metal buckles (Making Memories); cream tags (American Tag); fern punch (Carl); pine cone punch (Emagination Crafts); heart punch (EK Success); library pocket (Silver Bow Creations); tan, green, red and cream cardstocks; brad*

Faces of AJ

STAMP DESCRIPTIVE WORDS

To create her journaling words, Janetta began each word with a capital block letter for emphasis. Stamp block letters on white cardstock in black ink, spacing them far enough apart that there is room for the rest of each word. Stamp remainders of each word by combining upper- and lowercase letters. Trim words into rectangles, ink edges with black ink and adhere to page with brads. Stamp title words on white cardstock with brown, black and blue inks. Cut out and ink edges with brown ink.

Janetta Abucejo Wieneke, Memory Makers Books

Supplies: *Patterned papers (Carolee's Creations, DieCuts with a View, Keeping Memories Alive); Crayon Fun letter stamps (Stampin' Up!); Antique Alphabet letter stamps (EK Success); Holle's Inspiration letter stamps (Prickley Pear Rubber Stamps); Old Book letter stamps (Hampton Arts Stamps); Printer's and Alphabet Blocks letter stamps (Hero Arts); "Summer" stamp (Magnetic Poetry); date stamp (Making Memories); Ancient Page Chocolate and Vivid Storm Blue stamping inks (Clearsnap); black stamping ink (Stampabilities); blue brads (DieCuts with a View); light blue photo corners; black, brown, light blue and white cardstocks*

Love

STAMP INTO CRAFT FOAM

Jeniece stamped letters into craft foam sheets for an elegant and inviting title design. Ink a letter stamp with pink ink and set aside. Using a heat gun, warm a portion of a craft foam sheet and immediately stamp letter into it. Hold stamp in foam for a few seconds to allow the foam to cool. Heat the adjacent area of foam and repeat the process until the letters (both large and small) are completed. Cut out title and mount in the center of a white cardstock square. Surround with pink ribbon and buttons. Cut out smaller letters and adhere to piece of green ribbon as a way to embellish journaling. Using pink and green inks, stamp journaling and photo caption on patterned and pink papers in a variety of smaller styles.

Jeniece Higgins, Lake Forest, Illinois

Supplies: *Patterned papers (Anna Griffin, Rusty Pickle); white craft foam sheet (Darice); large negative image and tiny typewriter letter stamps (Ma Vinci's); small uppercase letter stamps (PSX Design); "&" block stamp and small letter stamps (Hero Arts); Image Tree curly letter stamps (EK Success); pink stamping ink (Tsukineko); rub-on letters and silk flower (Making Memories); pink label holder (Scrapworks); white cardstock; green ribbons; buttons; white embroidery floss*

Supplies: *Patterned papers (Creative Imaginations, K & Company, Karen Foster Design); brown liquid appliqué (Marvy); decorative buttons (K & Company); heart brad (Creative Imaginations); metal letters (Making Memories); letter stamps (Barnes & Noble); black stamping ink (Stampin' Up!); horseshoe die cut (Ellison); metallic rub-ons (Craf-T); white cardstock; walnut ink; denim fabric; thin chipboard; red leather lacing; star concho; bandanna fabric; belt buckle*

Hey Cowgirl

"BRAND" FAUX LEATHER

Tricia created faux leather hides for her title by stamping into hot liquid appliqué on chipboard. She used the same technique on a small photo frame to unify the page.

Tricia Rubens, Castle Rock, Colorado

STEP-BY-STEP: FAUX LEATHER STAMPING

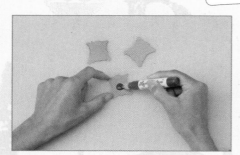

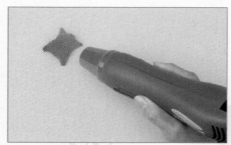

1 Cut shapes from chipboard for title letters. Apply liquid appliqué to shapes and spread around with fingertip to cover entire surface.

2 Heat liquid appliqué with embossing gun to achieve a raised, textured finish. The longer you heat, the lighter in color the finish will be.

3 Press letters into surface with black solvent ink to achieve the look of stamped leather.

Crew Cuts

COMBINE A BACKGROUND STAMP WITH A COMPUTER FONT

Using a single stamp, Shannon created patterns for letter outlines and their background blocks. Load stamp with black ink and press it onto white cardstock four times. Cut apart each stamped rectangle. Print title on turquoise cardstock and silhouette cut each letter. Place letters on scrap paper and stamp the same image in black on each letter, making sure that the letters fall in the center of the stamped design. Position and adhere stamped letters over background blocks so that the design appears to be continuous. Mat each stamped rectangle with red cardstock. Stamp a square tile covered in a turquoise rectangle in the same fashion to coordinate.

Shannon Taylor, Bristol, Tennessee

Supplies: *Mini squares stamp (Inkadinkado); StazOn black solvent ink (Tsukineko); acrylic buckle, white square tile and zipper pull tiles (Junkitz); red rub-on letters (Scrapworks); grosgrain ribbon (Offray); acrylic numbers (KI Memories); white, red and turquoise cardstocks; brads; hinges; black pen*

Create Art

STAMP INTO MODELING PASTE

Julie covered her background with modeling paste in order to stamp on a unique surface. Cover a piece of 12 x 12" illustration board with modeling paste. Use an old credit card to level the paste. While paste is still wet, dip foam letter stamps into water and then stamp into paste. Allow paste to dry. Rub two shades of yellow watercolor crayons onto a paint palette. Dip a foam brush in water and then in colors to paint the background (similar to painting with watercolor paints). Rub blue and purple watercolor crayons on palette and use a small paintbrush and water to color the insides of the letters. Stamp a swirl design in purple directly onto the page. Stamp journaling onto photo with black solvent ink.

Julie Geiger, Gold Canyon, Arizona

Supplies: *Illustration board (Nielsen & Bainbridge); heavy modeling paste (Liquitex); Evolution letter stamps, Jersey and Misunderstood foam letter stamps (Making Memories); swirl stamp (Rubber Stampede); dark yellow, yellow, blue and purple watercolor crayons (Loew Cornell); StazOn black solvent ink (Tsukineko); foam brush; watercolor paintbrush*

Supplies: Patterned paper and premade leather word (Rusty Pickle); Button letter stamps (PSX Design); uppercase letter stamps (Hero Arts); Dot letter and Susan Branch Manuscript letter stamps (All Night Media); Jive letter stamps (Stamp Craft); brown stamping ink (Stampin' Up!); embroidery floss; brown cardstock; brads

Celebrate

STAMP WORDS ON A COLLAGED BACKGROUND

Shannon created her card's background to mimic the look of a premade leather embellishment. Tear bits of brown patterned papers. Start by adhering the pieces at the top of the card and work down, overlapping each one. Lightly ink the collaged surface with brown. Mount a premade leather embellishment across the center of the card. Stamp words across the card background in brown ink using several letter stamp styles.

Shannon Taylor, Bristol, Tennessee

Happy Birthday to You

STAMP OVER DIFFERENT MEDIA

Polly gave all the simple stamped words on this birthday card a slightly different touch. Paint small portions of file folder-style card with yellow and purple paints. When dry, stamp words in black over the paint. Stamp other words in black on a small white tag and round vellum tag. Attach tags to page and accent words with small silk flower and buttons. Stamp smaller words on file folder tab.

Polly McMillan, Bullhead City, Arizona

Supplies: Letter stamps (Hero Arts, PSX Design); file folder card (Rusty Pickle); tags (Avery); ribbon (Offray); buttons (Making Memories); flowers (Wal-Mart); yellow and purple paints (Plaid); black stamping ink

Winner

STAMP ON WOVEN RIBBON AND GAME TICKETS

Melissa created a fun, game-themed card with a stamped title that appears to hold all the elements in place. Stamp word onto woven ribbon with black ink. Stamp on blank game tickets with several letter stamp styles and black ink. Ink edges of tickets. Adhere mini game embellishments and stamped tickets to popcorn bag and card base. With straight pins, attach ribbon and stamped title over embellishments.

Melissa Smith, North Richland, Texas

Supplies: *Word stamp (Ma Vinci's); game pieces, tickets, cards, popcorn bag and letter stamps (Leave Memories); green cardstock; black stamping ink; straight pins; gingham and woven ribbons*

Seasons Greetings

DRESS UP AN ORNAMENT STAMP

Words become a design element on Adrienne's card. Stamp ornament with tinted embossing ink on green cardstock. Heat emboss with gold powder. Cut out the image and tie on a ribbon. Thread a bead onto fiber and tie around top of ornament. Color copy a vintage postage stamp and attach to card with foam tape.

Adrienne Kennedy, My Sentiments Exactly
Colorado Springs, Colorado

Supplies: *Patterned papers (Anna Griffin); Ornament Sentiment stamp (My Sentiments Exactly); Top Boss tinted embossing ink (Clearsnap); red photo corners (Kolo); ribbon (May Arts); gold embossing powder (Tsukineko); red and green cardstocks; postage stamp; red bead; foam tape*

All of
God's grace
in one
little face

Nate ~ 3 years old
September 26, 2003

Chapter 4

Borders, Corners and Frames

Discover even more ways to adorn your pages by making stamped borders, corners and frames, featuring techniques such as stamping on paper piecing, stamping over photos, woven stamped borders, adding microscope slides to stamps and more. Find step-by-step ideas on:

My Family My Roots

EMBOSS WITH DIFFERENT POWDERS

Jodi added smooth elegance to her page with silver embossing powders. Cover a large slide mount with patterned paper to serve as a photo frame. Stamp on the frame using a clear embossing ink, then sprinkle with extra-fine silver powder and heat. Achieve smooth edges around the frame by generously inking the edges with clear ink and embossing them with silver extra thick embossing powder. Add a second layer around edges for extra texture. Use the same technique around edges of background, title and small slide mount.

Jodi Amidei, Memory Makers Books

Supplies: *Paisley patterned paper and transparency (Creative Imaginations); mesh (Magenta); slide mounts (Design Originals, Foofala); flower design stamp (Stampa Rosa); Ultra Thick Embossing Enamel platinum powder; clear embossing ink (Ranger); key charm (Jest Charming); wire-edged ribbon; wire; extra-fine silver embossing powder; blue and turquoise cardstocks; square brads; foam tape*

Celebrate

STAMP AN ELEGANT BORDER AND CORNERS

Corry used a variety of stamping and embossing techniques all across this spread for an elegant wedding layout. Stamp border pattern with green ink around several sides of cream cardstock background. Layer background with wide strip of red cardstock and stamp again along edge. Apply gold embossing powder to stamping on red and heat. Attach gold ribbon over gold embossing. For focal-point photo, round corners and mat on green patterned paper. Trim corners of mat with decorative corner punch and stamp accents in each corner. Emboss corners with gold powder. For title and decorated tag, stamp letters and flower accent into several layers of extra thick embossing powder with gold ink.

Corry Heinricks, Silver Valley, Alberta, Canada

Supplies: *Patterned paper (Anna Griffin); Gentler Times stamp set (Stampin' Up!); Playful acrylic letter stamps, Cranberry and Olive stamping inks (Close To My Heart); Colorbox gold stamping ink (Clearsnap); gold embossing powder (Stampendous!); VersaMark watermark ink (Tsukineko); clear Ultra Thick Embossing Enamel powder (Ranger); date stamp (Making Memories); corner punch scissors (Fiskars); square punch (Creative Memories); gold charm (from old jewelry); red and cream cardstocks; vellum; braided cord; fibers; gold photo corners gold sheer ribbon; skeleton leaf*

Supplies: *Patterned paper (Carolee's Creations); patterned tea bag folding paper (Design Originals); Long Life stamp (All Night Media); Open Weave texture stamp (PSX Design); green stamping ink (Anna Griffin); Colorbox Metallic Gold stamping ink (Clearsnap); EZ2Cut letter template (Accu-Cut); circle template (Fiskars); glitter spray and clear beads (Duncan); black, brown and sage cardstocks; green vellum*

Koi Fish

COMBINE PATTERNED PAPER WITH SMALL STAMPED ACCENTS

Beginning with patterned paper squares used for tea bag folding, Oksanna created a border. Mat two patterned squares with black paper; arrange squares across bottom of page. Stamp a round Chinese character for long life onto small squares of brown cardstock using green ink. Mat each square with sage green cardstock and adhere to patterned paper squares. Accent certain squares with small green vellum strips. For a subtle framing effect around one photo, stamp a square woven design two times on background paper with gold ink. Layer matted photo over parts of the design.

Oksanna Pope, Los Gatos, California

TIP: For even, precise shading of detailed stamps like the tiger's face, apply chalk inks with a foam finger dauber.

A Walk on the Wild Side

WEAVE STAMPED IMAGES

Jodi created an intricate woven border with just a few steps. With black ink, stamp and emboss a 4¼" wide strip of cream cardstock with tiger stripes. On another cream strip of the same width, stamp and emboss a tiger's face. Shade the face and between the stripes using chalk inks. Use a craft knife and ruler to make vertical slits ¼" apart along the entire width of the tiger stripes. Leave the top and bottom edges intact to assist in weaving. Cut tiger face piece horizontally into 1" strips except for the tiger's face. Weave the horizontal strips underneath the thin striped slits. For wider strip featuring tiger's face, weave over the slits.

Jodi Amidei, Memory Makers Books

Supplies: *Tiger stripes stamp (Rubberstamp Ave.); tiger face stamp (Embossing Arts Company); Ancient Page black stamping ink, Colorbox Yellow Ochre, Yellow Cadmium, Burnt Sienna and Peach Pastel cat eye chalk inks (Clearsnap); StazOn black solvent ink (Tsukineko); clear embossing ink (Ranger); black embossing powder (Stamp a Mania); black letter tiles (Westrim); stencil letter and square concho (Scrapworks); typewriter key conchos (Colorbök); rub-on letters (Making Memories); blender pen (ChartPak); square tiles (EK Success); black, brown, rust and cream cardstocks; patterned fabric; beads; black domino*

Looking Good in My Pink Summer Shades

STAMP A CHECKERBOARD BORDER

Using a square stamp she found in a letter set, Cindy created a checkerboard border pattern. Cut a 1" strip of white cardstock. Stamp squares in an alternating pattern in black ink, allowing the edges of the squares to touch the top and bottom edges of the strip. Ink the edges with black ink and shade with black chalk. Tie with black-and-white gingham ribbon to finish.

Cindy Harris, Modesto, California

Supplies: *Patterned paper (Mustard Moon); square stamp (Hero Arts); black stamping ink (Stampendous!); letter beads (Westrim); label holder stamp and letter stamps (River City Rubber Works); black wire mesh (Scrapyard 329); flower brads (Making Memories); white, pink and sage green cardstocks; gingham ribbon; wire; brads; small tag; chalk; black pen*

TIP: To keep pigment powders from wearing off stamped images over time, apply a spray fixative when finished.

Winter 2004

LAYER CUT-OUT ELEMENTS

Samantha's layered border gives the impression of falling snow. Using a snowflake-patterned roller stamp, apply watermark ink on blue and black cardstocks. Color the images with pigment powder using a soft-bristled brush. Trim stamped strip and adhere along left side of page. Stamp additional snowflakes in watermark ink and dust with pigment powders again. Cut out each snowflake. Layer individual snowflakes over stamped strip with foam tape. Add clear and pearl accents.

Samantha Walker, Battle Ground, Washington

Supplies: *Stampin' Around snowflake roller stamp and other snowflake stamps (Stampin' Up!); VersaMark watermark ink (Tsukineko); Pearl Ex silver, gold and rose metallic pigment powders (Jacquard Products); number stamps (source unknown); workable fixative spray (Krylon); metal strips (Making Memories); winter sticker (EK Success); silver trim (Fibre Craft); blue stamping ink; black, lavender, white and blue cardstocks; ribbon trim, metal label holder; pearl and clear accents; foam tape*

Supplies: *Patterned papers (Bo-Bunny Press); Antique Uppercase letter stamps (PSX Design); VersaMark watermark ink (Tsukineko); Delightful Doodles flower stamp, Old Olive, More Mustard, Really Rust stamping inks, clear embossing powder and clear lacquer (Stampin' Up!); fibers (Fibers By The Yard); metal letter charms (Making Memories); conchos (Scrapworks); round rub-on letters (Creative Imaginations); square punch (Creative Memories); orange, yellow, peach, ivory and green cardstocks; vellum; brads; sandpaper; sewing machine*

Summer Sizzle

ADD RESIST TECHNIQUES TO A BORDER AND FRAME

K'Lynne chose bright, warm colors for stamping and decorating a border, frame and accents on this summer-themed page. Begin by stamping flowers and words on orange cardstock with watermark ink and heat emboss with clear powder. To make the elements visible, sponge cardstock with several colored inks and wipe away from embossed images. Cut flower images into squares, mat with yellow and stitch to page over peach strip. Use other stamped flowers as accents. Trim word-embossed cardstock and use as a photo mat. To decorate metal letters, sand them and then cover with yellow ink. Sprinkle with clear embossing powder and heat.

K'Lynne Dunham, Cleburne, Texas

Vail

HIGHLIGHT A STAMPED BORDER WITH MICROSCOPE SLIDES

Clear microscope slides offer a slightly magnified appearance to stamped patterns. In dark blue and green inks, stamp various patterns over dark patterned paper. On lighter patterned paper using lighter ink shades, stamp the same images again. Trim the lighter patterns into thin rectangles and position over darker paper so the images appear continuous. Run lighter rectangles through an adhesive-application machine on both sides. Adhere over darker paper and press microscope slides over lighter paper rectangles.

Erikia Ghumm, Brighton, Colorado

Supplies: *Patterned papers, epoxy letter stickers and faux wax seal (Creative Imaginations); inkjet watercolor photo paper (Epson); leaf stamps (Stampendous!); Colorbox brown, green and blue fluid chalk inks (Clearsnap); green iridescent acrylic paint (Golden Artist Colors); adhesive-application machine (Xyron); decorative nailheads (JewelCraft); label maker (Dymo); white and green cardstocks; microscope slides; blue trim*

We will miss the gardens at our house in North Carolina so much! I think we had every color of Azalea. The first blooms each spring never stayed on long ~ you and Em always picked them and brought them to me!

Supplies: *Flower stamps and extra-fine black embossing powder (Creative Images Rubber Stamps); Colorbox purple and black stamping inks (Clearsnap); word stamps (Leave Memories); Twinkling H_2Os shimmering watercolor paints (LuminArte); transparency; brown, ivory, lavender and green cardstocks; purple, pink and green ribbons; heart pins; beads*

Bloom

MASK STAMPED IMAGES FOR A CONTINUOUS BORDER

Using black pigment ink, Melissa began by stamping and embossing one flower image on her background paper. To achieve the look that parts of certain flowers are hidden behind others, she employed a masking technique. After all images were stamped, Melissa filled in the stamped outlines with shimmering watercolor paints.

Melissa Smith, North Richland, Texas

STEP-BY-STEP: MASKED CORNERS

1 Stamp a flower image on cardstock with black ink. Photo copy the stamped image and cut out. Temporarily adhere the copied image over the stamped one.

2 With photocopied image over the stamped image, stamp second flower image next to the first, allowing one side to overlap. Remove the photocopy for the masked effect. Continue the process for masking other flowers.

TIP: When inking or painting an image with multiple colors, start with the lighter colors first, then blend in the darker shades.

Exploring the East Coast

REPEAT A STAMPED IMAGE

As they often do on the beach, rows of seagulls flock together on Holle's page border. Tear two strips of tan cardstock. Ink a seagulls stamp with black ink and press it several times across strips. Color the images with white pencil and orange and silver pens. Add black dots with pen around seagulls to resemble sand. For "sandy" background, crumple plastic wrap, dip into stamping ink and dab across pages.

Holle Wiktorek, Reunion, Colorado
Photos: Georgia Norman, Nashville, Tennessee

Supplies: *On the Beach stamp set, Basic Black, Caramel and Close to Cocoa stamping inks (Stampin' Up!); colored pencils and pens (EK Success); letter template (Wordsworth); rub-ons and clay phrase (Li'l Davis Designs); star brads (Creative Impressions); black, blue, red, cream and tan cardstocks; twill ribbon; white mulberry paper; star brads; foam tape; plastic wrap*

A Side Trip to Yelapa

LAYER STAMPED IMAGES FOR TEXTURE

Samantha gave her stamped shoreline border added interest by layering images with foam adhesive. Run roller stamp with brown ink across watercolor paper. Emboss with clear powder. Paint the border with watercolors. Roll another strip with roller stamp, emboss and cut out select shell images. Paint cut-outs and adhere over identical shells with foam tape. Tear top edge of watercolor paper and paint with blue to resemble water.

Samantha Walker, Battle Ground, Washington

Supplies: *Corrugated paper, straw mesh and aqua textured papers (FLAX art & design); patterned paper (Scrapworks); watercolor paper (Fabriano); By the Sea roller stamp, Close to Cocoa roller stamp cartridge, clear embossing powder, Tempting Turquoise, Only Orange and Brilliant Blue stamping inks (Stampin' Up!); title letters (from antique printer's type set); watercolor paints (Windsor & Newton); blue, turquoise, white and orange cardstocks; fabric; freshwater pearl beads; shells; button; decorative half pearls; sea glass and pottery; acrylic pebbles; hot glue; coral bead necklace; black pen; foam tape*

Celebrate

STAMP A COLOR-BLOCKED FRAME AND CORNER

Using primary colored inks, Michelle gave this spread a lively feel, appropriate for a boy's birthday. Stamp a happy birthday block stamp multiple times in four colors onto white cardstock. Tear around six squares and arrange on black cardstock. Trim edges of black to create photo mat. For corner accent, tear smaller squares in different colors from same block stamps. Mount on black and trim to fit corner. Accent frame and corner with puzzle pieces decorated with ink and metal words.

Michelle Keeth, Lowell, Arkansas

Supplies: *Patterned papers and paint chips (Daisy D's); birthday stamp (Hero Arts); red, yellow, green, blue and black stamping inks (Ranger, Tsukineko); metal words (Making Memories); puzzle piece letters (Li'l Davis Designs); letter stickers (Doodlebug Design, Pebbles); birthday themed tin tiles (Scrapyard 329); waxed twine (Scrapworks); jump rings (Junkitz), metal tag (Creative Impressions); blue, white and black cardstocks; brads; foam tape; black pen*

Happy Together

FRAME A PHOTO ENLARGEMENT

A thin, subtle black and white border keeps the focus on Linda's striking photo enlargement. Measure and trim white cardstock to fit behind photo enlargement. Using black ink, stamp a swirl pattern along top and bottom edges of white cardstock. Sprinkle with clear embossing powder and heat. Mat photo on stamped pattern, layering with thin strips of black cardstock. Stamp monogram in black, emboss and cut out with circle punch. Shade background of monogram with green ink and mat on black. For page background, lightly run green stamp pad across white textured cardstock until covered entirely. Stamp images in green across background.

Linda Beeson, Ventura, California

Supplies: *White textured cardstock (DMD); Encore Honeydew stamping ink (Tsukineko); Brilliance black stamping ink (Clearsnap); Imprintz silver embossing powder (Stewart Superior); Swirl stamp (Penny Black); wax seal stamp (Rubber Stamps of America); heart stamp (PSX Design); Love and Kisses stamp (Rubber Stampede); Victorian flourish stamps (Anna Griffin, All Night Media); script stamp (A Stamp in the Hand); letter stamps (Hero Arts); circle punch (Family Treasures); shrink plastic; black and white cardstocks; clear embossing powder*

Welcome to Paradise

COMBINE STAMPING INKS AND MARKERS

Samantha gives a photo more emphasis by framing it with stamped designs. Stamp frame on white cardstock with green ink. Color around edges of frame and within the design with a darker green marker. Stamp flowers on white cardstock with pink ink. Color around edges with a red marker and cut out. Do the same for leaves using green ink and markers. Apply clear embossing powder to flowers and leaves and heat. Layer around bottom of frame and attach with foam tape.

Samantha Walker, Battle Ground, Washington

Supplies: *Patterned paper and square conchos (Scrapworks); bark and grass papers (FLAX art & design); letter stamps, Framed Fun stamp set, Green Galore and Positively Pink stamping inks (Stampin' Up!); flower embellishment and red and green pens (EK Success); butter, red, melon, brown and white cardstocks; vellum; chalk; black pen; foam tape*

Supplies: Patterned papers
(K & Company); tan clay (Polyform
Products); celebrate stamp (Hero Arts);
letter stamps and decorative brads
(Making Memories); StazOn black
solvent ink (Tsukineko); metal keyhole
(Li'l Davis Designs); fibers; date stamp;
green and black cardstocks; lace trim;
sewing machine

Celebrate Christmas

TRANSFER A PHOTO ON A STAMPED CLAY FRAME

After stamping on clay, Andrea transferred a photo in the center of the clay to make it into a frame. She stamped a small clay tag with the same script stamp to coordinate.

Andrea Lyn Vetten-Marley, Aurora, Colorado

STEP-BY-STEP: CLAY FRAME PHOTO TRANSFER

1 Roll clay into a ball and flatten with rolling pin. Position color-copied photo you wish to transfer in center of clay. Using a stylus, make a guideline in clay that is ¼" larger than the photo itself. Remove photo. With black solvent ink, stamp around edges, allowing the images to fall inside the stylus outline.

2 Cut away excess clay on stylus guidelines to create frame. Replace color copy of photo face-down in the center of clay. Spray back with water and press down firmly. Bake according to package instructions, leaving photo in place.

3 When clay has cooled, spray back of photo with water again. Peel away damp paper backing with your fingers. Photographic image will have transferred onto the surface of the clay.

RUSH!
FREE ISSUE REQUEST!

BUSINESS REPLY MAIL
FIRST-CLASS MAIL   PERMIT NO. 347   FLAGLER BEACH FL

POSTAGE WILL BE PAID BY ADDRESSEE

MEMORY MAKERS
PO BOX 421400
PALM COAST FL 32142-7160

।।

Daddy Date Night
EMBOSS DIRECTLY ON A PHOTO

Laura used a frame stamp with journaling to high-light the subjects in her photo. Stamp frame directly on duplicate photograph with green ink. Sprinkle clear powder and heat emboss. Double mat photo with ivory and black cardstocks. Tear edges of black mat, apply ink and emboss edges.

Laura Stewart, Fort Wayne, Indiana

Supplies: *Patterned paper (Scrap Ease); letter die cuts (QuicKutz); frame stamp (Rubber Stampede); Colorbox green stamping ink (Clear-snap); clear embossing powder (Ranger); fleur de lis paper clips (Barnes & Noble), black and ivory cardstocks; black pen*

TIP: To ensure the photo will not be scorched during the embossing process, keep the heat gun farther away from the project than usual and move it around rapidly. In addition, avoid using high-temperature heat guns for this technique.

Fractured Fairy Tales

FEATURE A STAMPED, PAPER-PIECED AND BEADED FRAME

Tricia crafted a whimsical photo frame to accompany playful fairy tale-style journaling. Cut out frame shape and cover frame with bits of colored papers in various shapes. Stamp swirls with gold ink onto it. Cover frame with a strong, double-sided adhesive sheet and trim away the extra in the shape of the frame. Press clear tiny glass marbles onto the adhesive. Thread decorative beads onto wire and wrap wire around the frame.

Tricia Rubens, Castle Rock, Colorado

Supplies: *Patterned papers (SEI); letter stickers (Doodlebug Design); swirl stamps and gold stamping ink (Stampin' Up!); gold leafing pen (Krylon); tiny glass marbles (Art Accents); adhesive sheet (Magic Scraps); decorative glass beads (JewelCraft); gold frame (Nunn Design); clear plastic tile (Making Memories); white cardstock; buttons; wire*

Supplies: *Red and white velvets and holly leaf stamp (Hot Potatoes); gold border strip (Making Memories); decorative photo corners and jump rings (The Eggery Place); jingle bells (Crafts Etc.); holly and pine embellishment (Cottage Street Flowers); decorative washer (EK Success); black and gold tassels (Stampendous!): gold leafing pen (Krylon); Colorbox embossing ink (Clearsnap); Ultra Thick Embossing Enamel powder (Ranger); black Royal Coat Dimensional Magic paint (Plaid); black and green cardstocks; iron; spray bottle; foam tape*

Vision in Velvet

IRON IMAGES INTO VELVET

An embellished velvet frame provides the perfect setting for a holiday portrait of Denise's daughter. She stamped the background on white velvet using the same technique.

Denise Tucker, Versailles, Indiana

TIP: When purchasing velvet for the purpose of ironing shiny stamped impressions into it, look for acetate-rayon velvet.

STEP-BY-STEP: VELVET IMPRESSIONS

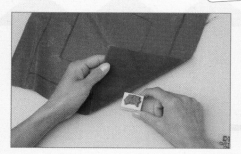

1 Trace frame's outline on the back of velvet. Place velvet right-side down on top of a rubber stamp. Mist velvet with water.

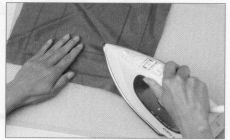

2 Make sure the stamp is placed inside the frame's outline. Position the iron so its steam holes are not located over the stamp. Press stamp into velvet. Be careful not to slide the iron.

3 Lift velvet to see impression. Repeat until area needed for frame is covered with images. Cut on guidelines and wrap velvet piece around a cardstock frame.

Backyard Oasis

COLOR STAMPS WITH MARKERS

Jodi used various colors of brush-tipped markers and a themed stamp set to create a border, frame and corners on this page. Color different parts of stamps with colored markers. "Huff" hot air on stamp immediately before stamping on page. Repeat coloring process inbetween each stamping. Stamp a border, frame and a variety of smaller accents on crackle patterned paper. Trim into a border strip and frame. To give the page dimension, cut out smaller stamped accents and attach to the border and frame with foam tape.

Jodi Amidei, Memory Makers Books

Supplies: *Tuscany stamp set (All Night Media); colored markers (Marvy); tan patterned paper (Hot Off The Press); crackle patterned paper (Provo Craft); brown cardstock; eyelets; ribbon; vellum; foam tape*

> **TIP:** When coloring stamps with brush markers containing dye ink, the ink may start to dry before you've applied it to paper. After coloring all parts of your stamp, remoisten the ink by exhaling hot air—known as "huffing"—onto the stamp before stamping.

Supplies: Patterned papers (Club Scrap, Sandylion, 7 Gypsies); silver script paper (source unknown); diamond stamp (Postmodern Design); diamond/square stamp (Stamp Barn); VersaMark watermark ink (Tsukineko); Adirondack Espresso stamping ink (Ranger); Chunky Copper embossing powder (B&J's Art Stamps); fibers; black cardstock

Faded Memories

CREATE FAUX COPPER EMBELLISHMENTS

Extra thick embossing powder in copper is the key ingredient for creating Jen's corner accents and embellishments on this reflective layout.

Jen Lowe, Lafayette, Colorado

STEP-BY-STEP: FAUX COPPER CORNERS

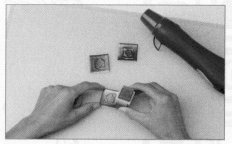

1 Press clear embossing ink pad on cardstock, sprinkle with bronze embossing powder and heat. Punch squares from embossed surface. Emboss enough surface to punch four squares.

2 Ink, sprinkle and heat emboss squares again for a thicker surface.

3 While embossed surface is still warm and soft, press in diamond stamp to create impression. Adhere squares at each corner of page.

Zest for Life

DRAW ATTENTION TO A PHOTO WITH CORNER STAMPS

Samantha used a sophisticated corner stamp to create a classic boy spread. Use a foam corner stamp and blue acrylic paint to stamp corner accents on rust cardstock. Double mat and mount photo in the center. Using a dry brush and more paint, swipe streaks of blue across the spread, bringing the two sides together.

Samantha Jackson, Belton, Texas

Supplies: *Patterned paper (Carolee's Creations); Philadelphia foam letter stamps, Corner foam dingbats stamps and Dusk Blue acrylic paint (Making Memories); small letter stamps (Rubber Stampede); rust and blue cardstocks; vellum; star brad*

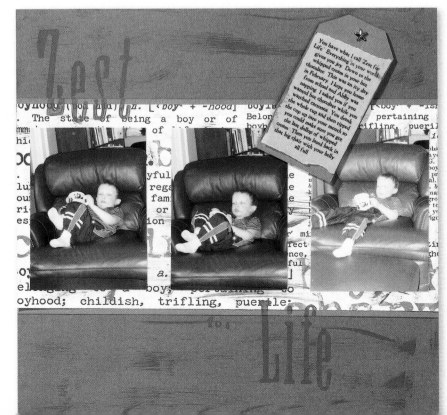

With All My Heart

STAMP ON PAINTED CANVAS

Melanie decorated frames and corners on this layout to highlight a loving relationship. Paint plain canvas with red acrylic paint. Let it dry and cover the canvas with several stamps loaded with black solvent ink. For smooth edges on the frame, trim the canvas, fold edges under and tape down. Adhere frame over focal-point photo. Stamp the same images in black on red cardstock photo mats. For decorative corners, dab white modeling paste through a brass stencil on red cardstock.

Melanie Douthit, West Monroe, Louisiana

Supplies: *Patterned papers (7 Gypsies); rub-on letters (Making Memories); date stamp (Stockwell); red paint (Plaid); heart swirl stamp (Rubber Stampede); antique key and Poste stamps (Stampabilities); map stamp (Hero Arts); StazOn black solvent ink (Tsukineko); brass corner stencil (Anna Griffin); modeling paste (Liquitex); polka-dot ribbon (Hobby Lobby); canvas fabric; brown and red cardstocks; brads; packing tape*

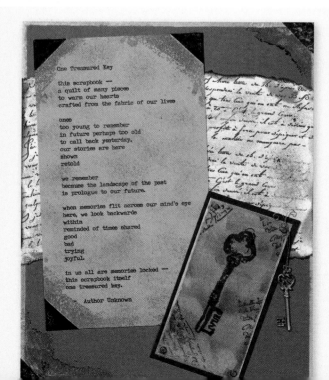

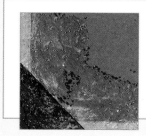

TIP: The amount of time that heat is applied to extra thick embossing powder will result in different effects. Less heating time produces smooth surfaces, while more heat results in bubbled effects. For even more dramatic looks, experiment with scorching the powder.

One Treasured Key

ACCENTUATE CORNERS WITH EXTRA THICK EMBOSSING POWDER

To coordinate with the stamped key and script images on her title page, Sharon embossed the corners of her layout and poem with clear extra thick embossing powder. Rub a glue stick over corners of layout and journaling block, being careful not to leave large globs of glue. Pour embossing powder over glue, shake off excess and heat.

Sharon Bissett O'Neal, Lee's Summit, Missouri

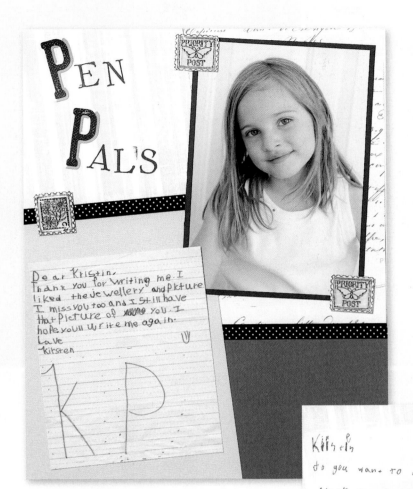

PEN PALS

Dear Kristin,
Thank you for writing me. I
liked the jewellery and picture.
I miss you too and I still have
that picture of you. I
hope youll write me again.
Love
Kirsten

KP

Kristin
do you want to be pinpals?
thank you for the letter
it's cool that where
doing this. my mom gave
me anether picterie of you
love, kristin

Kristin Thompson and Kirsten Petersen have been
pen-pals since they first met a couple of years ago.
Their moms are good friends, and it only seemed
natural that the girls would hit it off, too. The girls
got to meet for the first time about a year ago, and
have been writing back and forth ever since.

Nearly the same age and very similar in looks, they
could almost be mistaken for sisters. Instead, they
share a long-distance friendship that will hopefully
span the test of time.

Pictures Taken 2004

Pen Pals

COVER STAMPED EMBELLISHMENTS
WITH EPOXY STICKERS

Becky added details to the corners of her photos by
adding postage stamp embellishments for a cor-
respondence-themed page. Using black solvent ink,
stamp postage images onto patterned paper. Cover
images with clear epoxy stickers. Trim around the
stamped design and adhere at corners of photos and
other areas of the page.

Becky Thompson, Fruitland, Idaho
Photo: April Petersen, West Valley, Utah

Supplies: *Patterned papers (Creative Imaginations, Rusty Pickle);
Mail Art stamps kit (Hero Arts); StazOn black solvent ink
(Tsukineko); polka-dot border stickers (EK Success); clear epoxy
stickers (Making Memories); Road Trip letter stickers (Sticker Studio);
Piccadilly Uppercase letter stamps (PSX Design); pink, black and
brown cardstocks; memorabilia*

6 Months

CREATE CLAY CORNERS

Using a negative image stamp, Jeniece accented this baby portrait with corner embellishments made from clay. Form a ball from clay and roll out into a thin layer. Press stamp into air-dry clay four times. Cut out the images with a clay knife. Embellish each corner brushing blue paint over the raised areas with a dry brush. When paint dries, mount on each corner of the page.

Jeniece Higgins, Lake Forest, Illinois

Supplies: *Patterned papers (Provo Craft, Rusty Pickle); corner stamp (Stampabilities); letter stamps (PSX Design); Makin's clay, clay tools and baby charms (Provo Craft); rub-on letters and date stamps (Making Memories); number stencil (Ma Vinci's); Regency Blue paint (Plaid); blue and white cardstocks; fibers; ribbons; clock charm; sewing machine*

Always Questioning

DECORATE CORNER ACCENTS WITH WATER COLORS

Jen's feminine and imaginative corner designs coordinate well with a variety of preprinted paper accents. Press bird and flower stamp on white cardstock with black ink. Sprinkle with clear embossing powder and heat. Cut out the images. Use a small brush to color the images with watercolor paints. Add clear lacquer over the images. Adhere to the corners of the page.

Jen Lowe, Lafayette, Colorado

Supplies: *Patterned papers (Cross-My-Heart, Making Memories); preprinted die cuts (Cross-My-Heart); Turtledove stamp (Stamp Oasis); Colorbox black stamping ink (Clearsnap); clear embossing powder (Ranger); crystal lacquer (Sakura Hobby Craft); watercolor paints; ribbon; rose button; rose embellishment; vellum; green sheer ribbon*

Torla Tucker

...so many treasures waiting to be discovered.

EXPLORING

PARADISE

July 2004

Emerald Isle NC

Exploring Paradise

STAMP CORNER ACCENTS ON TWILL TAPE

Denise used two different widths of twill tape to stamp a title and photo corners. For corners, stamp black ink on wide ecru twill. Cut out corners and shade with pink and blue stamping inks. Stamp a title onto ½" pink twill.

Denise Tucker, Versailles, Indiana

Supplies: Patterned papers (Rusty Pickle); large corner stamp (Embossing Arts Co.); small corner stamp (Stampin' Up!); letter stamps (PSX Design); Colorbox blue and pink stamping inks (Clearsnap); Memories black stamping ink (Stewart Superior); metal border strip (Making Memories); pink and ecru twill tape (Creek Bank Creations); silk flowers (Cottage Street Flowers); clear Ultra Thick Embossing Enamel powder (Ranger); fabric; black and white cardstocks; transparency; starfish embellishment; brads; foam tape

TIP: To keep the stamped images looking crisp on twill, be careful not to use too much ink, and use a fast drying dye-based or solvent variety.

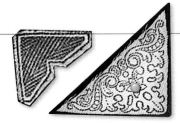

Happiness

EMBOSS A FRAME MULTIPLE TIMES

Erikia decorated a frame in a vintage style to complement her photo. Cover stamps with watermark ink, press on large slide mount and heat emboss with clear powder. Use ink pads to apply two colors over the embossed images. Wipe the images to clear away extra ink. Sprinkle clear powder across entire slide mount and emboss again. To darken the bright ink colors, cover it with black ink and rub most of it off. Emboss slide mount a third time with clear powder for the final layer.

Erikia Ghumm, Brighton, Colorado
Photo: Ken Trujillo, Memory Makers Photographer

Supplies: *Slide mount (Foofala); tiki stamp (Erikia's own design); script stamp (Hero Arts); Colorbox Dark Peony, Yellow Cadmium chalk inks and clear embossing powder (Clearsnap); copper tag (K & Company); hinge and key hole stickers (Creek Bank Creations); wire; brads; transparency*

Supplies: *London Bridge, Eiffel Tower and "A" background stamps (Stampington & Company); back text stamp (A Stamp In The Hand); Classic Caps letter stamp set (Hero Arts); 1 Montagerie Tea Bag Folding Cube corner stamps (Impression Obsession); Tin Can Mail Sun Dial clock stamp (Inkadinkado); Nick Bantock Cerulean Azure, Van Dyke Brown and Vermillion Lacquer stamping inks (Ranger); Memories black stamping ink (Stewart Superior); Colorbox Warm Red, Yellow Ochre and Amber Clay chalk inks (Clearsnap); clear lacquer (Sakura Hobby Craft); stipple brush; flat-edged paint brush; brown, black and cream cardstocks*

Bon Voyage

FRAME A STAMP WITH MORE STAMPS

For a travel-themed card, Colleen framed a stamped center image with even more coordinating stamps. Stamp the center image on cream cardstock with black ink. With red chalk ink, stamp words across the image. Apply blue ink near the top and yellow near the bottom with a stipple brush, blending the two colors at the center. On a 6½ x 4¾" rectangle of brown cardstock, stamp tea bag folding insignia on each corner in black ink. Fill in spaces between corners with an assortment of other stamps. Add slight red and yellow tints over the images with stamping inks and a stipple brush. Cut out center of brown cardstock to allow space for bridge image. Layer bridge image and frame over black card base. Coat stamped images with clear lacquer using a paint brush and let dry overnight.

Colleen Macdonald, Winthrop, Australia

Happy Birthday

STAMP CORNER ACCENTS ON A TRANSPARENCY

Shannon melds soft shades with stamping and painting on this birthday card. Lightly paint pink paper with blue color wash paint so that some of the paper shows through. Trim a transparency sheet to fit card, stamp angel images with black solvent ink and adhere to card. Layer with peach and striped papers and green ribbon. Shade a stencil letter with chalk, cover it with extra thick embossing powder and heat set. To finish, stamp birthday letters along the bottom in black ink.

Shannon Taylor, Bristol, Tennessee

Supplies: *Patterned paper (Kopp Design); "Happy" stencil letter (Autumn Leaves); green ribbon (Making Memories); blue paint (7 Gypsies); transparency (Creative Imaginations); angel stamp (Victorian Paper Co.); Ultra Thick Embossing Enamel clear powder (Ranger); Hopeless Heart letter stamps (FontWerks); peach and pink cardstocks; chalk*

TIP: To achieve a faded or aged look when pressing stamps to paper, stamp images on scrap paper first to remove some of the ink.

Supplies: *Newsprint patterned paper (source unknown); brown patterned paper (PSX Design); key hole stamps (Just For Fun); padlock cube stamp (Impression Obsession); letter stamps (Wordsworth); Memories black stamping ink (Stewart Superior); Nick Bantock Van Dyke Brown and Vermillion Lacquer stamping inks (Ranger); letter stickers (Provo Craft); gold cardstock; brads*

Dad

CREATE A BORDER STRIP WITH THEMED STAMPS

Various padlocks and key hole stamps on both the background and a border strip give Colleen's card a cohesive look. On gold card, stamp images in brown ink at various angles. Ink edges of card with brown. For border, tear a strip of brown patterned paper. Stamp key hole images in a straight line across the strip using black ink. Ink edges with brown. Attach strip to card with brads.

Additional Instructions and Credits

PAGE INSTRUCTIONS AND SOURCES

THE WORLD AWAITS COVER

Jodi's cover art melds stamping and weaving with colorful fabric accents. Stamp green background with watermark ink. On pink cardstock, stamp and heat emboss pattern with black powder. Tear edges of pink and mat on black. Stamp another pattern on darker green cardstock and emboss with gold powder. Cut gold embossed cardstock into 2½" squares; mount squares on pink. For woven tiles and title word, start by inking white cardstock with various colors. Cut inked cardstock into thin strips. Weave strips in a random fashion. Place woven strips over small tag board squares, cut slightly larger than square, wrap woven strips around tag board and adhere to back. Stamp each woven square with a leaf stamp. For title, stamp with letter stamps in black. Apply clear embossing ink to woven squares, sprinkle on clear embossing powder and heat emboss. Mount woven squares and title word to page with foam tape.

Jodi Amidei, Memory Makers Books

Supplies: *Leaf stamp (EK Success); background pattern stamps (All Night Media); letter stamps (Hampton Art, Hero Arts, My Sentiments Exactly); Colorbox stamping inks (Clearsnap); StazOn, VersaFine and VersaMark stamping inks (Tsukineko); Pinata stamping inks (Jacquard Products); paint pen (Sanford); wood slide mount (Li'l Davis Designs); pink square tiles (Little Black Dress Designs); eyelets (Making Memories); rectangle tile (Junkitz); gold, black and clear embossing powders (Stamp A Mania); thread; transparency; green, black and pink cardstocks; patterned fabric; foam tape*

BOOKPLATE P. 3

Stamp flower images at random on glossy paper; emboss with black powder. Apply colored stamping inks over remainder of glossy paper. Stamp and emboss other flowers on white cardstock, cut into squares and ink edges with magenta ink. Ink edges of larger cardstock square and mount all pieces on black. Mat black on white, inking edges, and adhere to glossy paper with foam tape.

Jodi Amidei, Memory Makers Books

Supplies: *Flower stamps (Kodomo); Ancient Page colored stamping inks (Clearsnap); clear embossing ink and glossy paper (Ranger); black embossing powder (Stamp A Mania); eyelets (Creative Impressions); ribbon (May Arts); white and black cardstocks*

MEOW P. 6

Jodi gave detailed cat stamps even more interest with several different techniques. Stamp large napping cat image on white watercolor paper with black ink. Color image with water color paints. Outline books on shelf with a gold pen. Cut image vertically in three equal sections. Cover sections with clear powder and heat emboss. Mat each section on black cardstock, then mat all three on larger piece of gold cardstock. For title, stamp four cat images in black ink on gold cardstock. Stamp four more cats on white cardstock and paint with watercolors. Stamp letters on painted cats and outline letters with clear lacquer. Silhouette cut all cats. Place finished cats on top of gold cats and adhere slightly off-center with foam tape.

Jodi Amidei, Memory Makers Books

Supplies: *Napping cat stamp (Stamps Happen); cat stamp (Stampabilities); letter stamps (Hero Arts); VersaMark and VersaFine stamping inks (Tsukineko); sepia stamping ink (Ranger); gold pen (Staedtler); bottle caps and stickers (Design Originals); clear lacquer (Plaid); paint pen (Krylon); vellum quote (Memories Complete); water color paints (Canson); charms;*

OUR VALENTINE SWEETHEART P. 12

Andrea stamped on clay to create embellishments that look like stone. To add to the stone look, she stamped her title on pieces of clay as well, and painted metal corner and border accents. Condition clay according to package directions. Roll flat to approximately ⅛" thick and place on a piece of foil. Stamp images onto clay with black ink and cut into heart shapes with cookie cutter. Remove excess clay from around heart-shaped piece carefully. For title, roll out excess clay into irregular shapes and stamp with letters. Place stamped images over foil on a cookie sheet and bake according to package directions.

Andrea Lyn Vetten-Marley, Aurora, Colorado

Supplies: *Letter stamps and metal embellishments (Making Memories); flower stamp (PSX Design); StazOn black stamping ink (Tsukineko); paint (Plaid); clay (Polyform Products); blue and black textured cardstocks (Bazzill)*

TOO BIG P. 36

Christine chose to mimic the fabric of "big" shorts with flower and leaf stamps. Use two types of ink to randomly stamp the images on a blue background. First stamp with watermark ink to deepen the blue color and then stamp with white ink for contrast.

Christine Penaflor, Fallbrook, California

Supplies: *White stamping ink, white embossing powder, Beautiful Batik flower, border and leaf stamps (Stampin' Up!); antique letter stamps (PSX Design); letter stamps (Wordsworth); VersaMark watermark ink (Tsukineko); label maker (Dymo); photo corner die cuts (QuicKutz); green ribbon (Offray); navy, blue and white cardstocks; vellum; foam tape*

PRACTICE HARD P. 60

Cynde combined various inking and painting techniques for different lettering elements. With green acrylic paint, stamp large foam letters on black cardstock for title. Next, paint metal letters and stamp a letter on each one with black solvent ink. Paint metal letters black, then sand for a distressed look.

Cynde Sharrock, Oak Ridge, Missouri

Supplies: *Patterned paper, label holder and preprinted transparency (Creative Imaginations); foam stamps, green paint, journaling definitions, metal star, star ribbon charm, metal letter charms, square metal tiles and brads (Making Memories); StazOn black solvent ink (Tsukineko); green twill (Creek Bank Creations); Colorbox gray chalk ink (Clearsnap); black and green cardstocks; embroidery floss; sandpaper*

ALL OF GOD'S GRACE P. 86

Nancy used a tri-color stamp pad to make the leaves on her page appear more realistic. First ink a leaf stamp with a spectrum ink pad in yellow, gold and orange and add green ink. Stamp randomly on a tan strip of cardstock. To create a stamped faux metal charm, apply several layers of gold embossing powder to a cardstock square. Melt powder with heat gun and while it is still hot, stamp in the leaf image. Allow the piece to cool slightly before lifting the stamp.

Nancy Kliewer, Fairfax, Virginia

Supplies: *Botanicals leaf stamp, letter stamps, Mellow Moss stamping ink, Pumpkin Patch Spectrum stamping ink and Gold Glaze embossing powder (Stampin' Up!); green, rust and tan cardstocks; paper crimper; green pen*

STAMP SOURCES
(SHOWN AS DESIGN ELEMENTS)

P. 1
3 Flowers: Stampendous!
My Mother's Dress: Inkadinkado
Etruscan Vine: Stampin' Up!
Eyeglasses: Just For Fun Rubber Stamps

P. 4
3 Flowers: Stampendous!
My Mother's Dress: Inkadinkado
Etruscan Vine: Stampin' Up!
Eyeglasses: Just For Fun Rubber Stamps
Eiffel Tower: Rubberstamp Ave.
Buttons: Serendipity Stamps
Spots with Dots: JudiKins
Circular Plaid Background: Savvy Stamps
Terrific Textures Crackle: PSX Design
Small Dot Pattern: Impress Rubber Stamps

P. 5
"R": Serendipity Alphabet & Numbers by Hero Arts
"G": Vintage Alphabet Stamps: Breite Italienne by Chronicle Books
"A": Typewriter Keys by Prickley Pear Rubber Stamps
"e": Retro Collection by Stampin' Up!
"X": All Caps Graphic Style Set by Scrappy Cat
Decorative Corner: PSX Design
Retro Squares from Retro Pattern Border Style Set: Rubber Stampede
Decorative Border: DeNami Design
Harlequin Frame: All Night Media
Corner Ornament: Magenta

P. 6
Old Typewriter: River City Rubber Works
3 Flowers: Stampendous!
Harlequin Frame: All Night Media
"m": Circle Pop Alphabet by Hero Arts
Corner Ornament: Magenta
Playing Cards: Just For Fun Rubber Stamps
"v": Alphabet Fun Lower by Stampin' Up!
Retro Squares from the Retro Pattern Borders Style Set: Rubber Stampede

P. 7
Lined Background: Magenta
Flower: Stars & Stamps
Animal Print: Stampendous!
Etruscan Grape: Stampin' Up
Moments Background: Hero Arts

P. 10
Playing Cards: Just For Fun Rubber Stamps
"B": Clear Set Alphabet Vintage Large Upper Case by River City Rubber Works
Eiffel Tower: Rubberstamp Ave.
Anna Griffin's Georgian Cartouche; All Night Media
Squiggle Line from Susy Ratto's Celebration 4 Piece Rubber Stamp Set: EK Success
Decorative Corner: PSX Design
Old Typewriter: River City Rubber Works

Animal Print: Stampendous!

"T": Mini Alphabets, Curlz by Hampton Art Stamps

Wavy Lines from Retro Pattern Border Style Set:
Rubber Stampede

Decorative Border: DeNami Design

Retro Squares from the Retro Pattern Border Style Set:
Rubber Stampede

"v": Alphabet Fun Lower by Stampin' Up!

"X": All Caps Graphic Style Set by Scrappy Cat

PP. 12-13

My Mother's Dress: Inkadinkado

Eyeglasses: Just For Fun Rubber Stamps

Old Typewriter: River City Rubber Works

Etruscan Vine: Stampin' Up!

Playing Cards: Just For Fun Rubber Stamps

Flower: Stars & Stamps Forever

Etruscan Grapes: Stampin' Up!

3 Flowers: Stampendous!

Eiffel Tower: Rubberstamp Ave.

PP. 16, 22, 24, 30, 32

Eiffel Tower: Rubberstamp Ave.

Eyeglasses: Just For Fun Rubber Stamps

Flower vine: Stars & Stamps Forever

Polar Bear Postage: Rubber Monger

PP. 36-37

Buttons: Serendipity Stamps

Terrific Textures Crackle: PSX Design

Diamond Pattern: Impress Rubber Stamps

Moments Background: Hero Arts

Small Dot Pattern: Impress Rubber Stamps

Circular Plaid background: #372e Savvy Stamps

Trifle Blocks: DeNami Design

Lined Background: Magenta

Animal print: Stampendous!

P. 39

Animal Print: Stampendous!

PP. 40, 42, 46, 48, 52, 58

Animal Print: Stampendous!

Buttons: Serendipity Stamps

Diamond Pattern: Impress Rubber Stamps

Small Dot Pattern: Impress Rubber Stamps

PP. 60-61

"v": Alphabet Fun Lower by Stampin' Up!

"S": Alphabet Fun Upper by
Stampin' Up!

"B": Clear Set Alphabet Vintage Large
Upper Case by River City Rubber Works

"R": Serendipity Alphabet & Numbers by Hero Arts

"A": Typewriter Keys by Prickley Pear Rubber Stamps

"W": Friendship Alphabet by
Hero Arts

"e": Retro collection by Stampin' Up!

"G": Vintage Alphabet Stamps Breite
Italienne by Chronicle Books

"T": Mini Alphabets, Curlz by Hampton
Art Stamps

"m": Circle Pop Alphabet by Hero Arts

"X": All Caps Graphic Style set by Scrappy Cat

Scrappy Cat

"m": Circle Pop Alphabet by Hero Arts

"B": Clear Set Alphabet Vintage Large
Upper Case by River City Rubber Works

"G": Vintage Alphabet Stamps Breite
Italienne by Chronicle Books

"A": Typewriter Keys by Prickley Pear Rubber Stamps

"R": Serendipity Alphabet & Numbers by Hero Arts

"e": Retro Collection by Stampin' Up!

"v": Alphabet Fun Lower by Stampin' Up!

P. 86

Retro Squares from the Retro Pattern Border Style set:
Rubber Stampede

Anna Griffin's Georgian Cartouche: All Night Media

Record Border: Just For Fun Rubber Stamps

Squiggle Line from Susy Ratto's Celebration 4 Piece Rubber
Stamp Set: EK Succes

Harlequin Frame: All Night Media

Curvy Lines from Retro Pattern Border Style Set:
Rubber Stampede

Decorative Border: DeNami Design

Decorative Corner: PSX Design

Corner Ornament: Magenta

PP. 92, 96, 98, 100

Retro Squares from the Retro Pattern
Border Style set: Rubber Stampede

Record Border: Just For Fun Rubber Stamps

Decorative Corner: PSX Design

Harlequin Frame: All Night Media

Anna Griffin's Georgian Cartouche: All Night Media

Corner Ornament: Magenta

SOURCE GUIDE

The following companies manufacture products featured
in this book. Please check your local retailers to find
these materials, or go to a company's Web site for the
latest product. In addition, we have made every attempt
to properly credit the items mentioned in this book. We
apologize to any company that we have listed incor-
rectly, and we would appreciate hearing from you.

3M
(800) 364-3577, www.3m.com

7 Gypsies
(800) 588-6707, www.7gypsies.com

Above the Mark
(530) 666-6648, www.abovethemark.com

Accu-Cut®
(800) 288-1670, www.accu-cut.com

All My Memories
(888) 553-1998, www.allmymemories.com

All Night Media (see Plaid Enterprises)

American Art Stamp
(310) 371-6593, www.americanartstamp.com

American Crafts
(801) 2226-0747, www.americancrafts.com

American Tag Co.
(800) 223-3956, www.americantag.net

American Tombow,Inc.
(800) 835-3232, www.tombowusa.com

Angel Company™, The (TAC)
(785) 820-9181, www.theangelcompany.net

Anna Griffin, Inc. (wholesale only)
(888) 817-8170, www.annagriffin.com

Art Impressions
(800) 393-2014, www.artimpressions.com

ARTchix Studio
(250) 370-9985, www.artchixstudio.com

Artistic Expressions
(219) 764-5158, www.artisticexpressionsinc.com

Autumn Leaves (wholesale only)
(800) 588-6707, www.autumnleaves.com

Avery Dennison Corporation
(800) GO-AVERY, www.avery.com

B & J's Art Stamps—no contact info

Barnes & Noble
www.barnesandnoble.com

Bazzill Basics Paper
(480) 558-8557, www.bazzillbasics.com

Be Unique
(909) 927-5357, beunique001@yahoo.com

Beadworks®
(800) 232-3761, www.beadworks.com

Blumenthal Lansing
(201) 935-6220, www.buttonsplus.com

Bo-Bunny Press
(801) 771-4010, www.bobunny.com

Boutique Trims, Inc.
(248) 437-2017, www.boutiquetrims.com

Buttons Galore
(856) 753-0165, www.buttonsgaloreandmore.com

Canson®, Inc.
(800) 628-9283, www.canson-us.com

Card Connection—see Michaels

CARL Mfg. USA, Inc.
(800) 257-4771, www.Carl-Products.com

Carolee's Creations®
(435) 563-1100, www.ccpaper.com

Carolines—no contact info

ChartPak
(800) 628-1910, www.chartpak.com

Chatterbox, Inc.
(208) 939-9133, www.chatterboxinc.com

Chronicle Books
(800) 722-6656, www.chroniclebooks.com

Clearsnap, Inc.
(360) 293-6634, www.clearsnap.com

Close To My Heart®
(888) 655-6552, www.closetomyheart.com

Club Scrap™, Inc.
(888) 634-9100, www.clubscrap.com

Cock-A-Doodle Design, Inc.
(800) 954-0559, www.cockadoodledesign.com

Colorbök™, Inc. (wholesale only)
(800) 366-4660

Cottage Street Flowers—no contact info

Craf-T Products
(507) 235-3996, www.craf-tproducts.com

Crafts, Etc. Ltd.
(800) 888-0321, www.craftsetc.com

Creative Images Rubber Stamps
(877) 406-5065, www.cistamps.com

Creative Imaginations
(800) 942-6487, www.cigift.com

Creative Memories®
(800) 468-9335, www.creativememories.com

Creative Paperclay Company®
(805) 484-6648, www.paperclay.com

Creative Papers Online Handmade Paper
(800) PAPER-40, www.handmade-paper.us

Creek Bank Creations, Inc.
(217) 427-5980, www.creekbankcreations.com

Cross-My-Heart-Cards, Inc.
(888) 689-8808, www.crossmyheart.com

C-Thru® Ruler Company, The (wholesale only)
(800) 243-8419, www.cthruruler.com

Daffodil Hill—no contact info

Daisy D's Paper Company
(888) 601-8955, www.daisydspaper.com

Darice, Inc.
(800) 321-1494, www.darice.com

DecoArt™, Inc.
(800) 367-3047, www.decoart.com

Delta Technical Coatings, Inc.
(800) 423-4135, www.deltacrafts.com

Deluxe Designs
(480) 205-9210, www.deluxedesigns.com

DeNami Design Rubber Stamps
(253) 437-1626, www.denamidesign.com

Derwent Cumberland Pencil Co.
www.pencils.co.uk

Design Originals
(800) 877-0067, www.d-originals.com

DieCuts with a View™
(877) 221-6107, www.dcwv.com

DMD Industries, Inc. (wholesale only)
(800) 805-9890, www.dmdind.com

Doodlebug Design™ Inc.
(801) 966-9952, www.doodlebugdesinginc.com

Dreamweaver Stencils
(909) 824-8343, www.dreamweaverstencils.com

Duncan Enterprises
(800) 782-6748, www.duncan-enterprises .com

Dymo
www.dymo.com

Eberhard Faber, makers of FIMO
www.eberhardfaber.de

Eggery Place, The
www.theeggeryplace.com

EK Success™, Ltd. (wholesale only)
(800) 524-1349, www.eksuccess.com

Ellison® Craft & Design
(800) 253-2238, www.ellison.com

Emagination Crafts, Inc. (wholesale only)
(630) 833-9521, www.emaginationcrafts.com

Embellished Girl, The—no contact info

Embossing Arts Company
(800) 662-7955, www.embossingarts.com

Epson America, Inc.
www.epson.com

Fabriano—no contact info

Family Treasures, Inc.®
www.familytreasures.com

Fanciruls, Inc.
(607) 849-6870, www.fancifulsinc.com

Fibers by the Yard™
(405) 364-8066, www.fibersbytheyard.com

Fibre-Craft®
www.fibrecraft.com

Fiskars, Inc. (wholesale only)
(715) 842-2091, www.fiskars.com

FLAX art & design
(415) 552-2355, www.flaxart.com

FontWerks
www.fontwerks.com

FoofaLa
(402) 758-0863, www.foofala.com

Fox River Paper Co.—no contact info

Frances Meyer, Inc.®
(800) 372-6237, www.francesmeyer.com

Fruit Basket Upset—no contact info

Golden Artist Colors, Inc.
(800) 959-6543, www.goldenpaints.com

Halcraft USA
212) 376-1580, www.halcraft.com

Hampton Art Stamps, Inc.
(800) 229-1019, www.hamptonart.com

H.E. Harris & Co.®
(a division of Whitman Publishing, LLC)
(800) 564-2995, www.WhitmanBooks.com

Heart Patch Craft—no contact info

Hearty—no contact info

Hero Arts® Rubber Stamps, Inc.
(800) 822-4376, www.heroarts.com

Hirschberg Schutz & Co., Inc.
(800) 221-8640

Hobby Lobby Stores, Inc.
www.hobbylobby.com

Home Depot U.S.A., Inc.
www.homedepot.com

Hot Off The Press, Inc.
(800) 227-9595, www.paperpizazz.com

Hot Potatoes
(615) 296-8002, www.hotpotatoes.com

Impress Rubber Stamps
(206) 901-9101, www.impressrubberstamps.com

Impression Obsession
(877) 259-0905, www.impression-obsession.com

Inkadinkado® Rubber Stamps
(800) 888-4652, www.inkadinkado.com

Jacquard Products/Rupert, Gibbon, & Spider, Inc.
(800) 442-0455, www.jacquardproducts.com

Jesse James & Co., Inc.
(610) 435-0201, www.jessejamesbutton.com

Jest Charming
(702) 564-5101, www.jestcharming.com

JewelCraft LLC
(201) 223-0804, www.jewelcraft.biz

Jo Sonja's, Inc.
(888) JOSONJA, www.josonja.com

Jo-Ann Fabric & Crafts
(888) 739-4120, www.joann.com

Joy of Stamping, a division of Pacific Products
(209) 267-9134, www.joyofstamping.com

JudiKins
(310) 515-1115, www.judikins.com

Just For Fun® Rubber Stamps
(727) 938-9898, www.jffstamps.com

K & Company
(888) 244-2083, www.kandcompany.com

Karen Foster Design (wholesale only)
(801) 451-9779, www.karenfosterdesign.com

Keeping Memories Alive™
(800) 419-4949, www.scrapbooks.com

Keepsake Designs—no contact info

KI Memories
(972) 243-5595, www.kimemories.com

Kodomo, Inc.
(650) 589-8681, www.kodomoinc.com

Kolo®, LLC
(888) 636-5656, www.kolo-usa.com

Kopp Design
(801) 489-6011, www.koppdesign.com

Krylon
(216) 566-200, www.krylon.com

La Pluma, Inc.
(615) 273-7367, www.debrabeagle.com

Lasting Impressions for Paper, Inc.
(801) 298-1979, www.lastingimpressions.com

Leave Memories
(518)281-4393, www.leavememories.com

Li'l Davis Designs
(949) 838-0344, www.lildavisdesigns.com

Limited Edition Rubberstamps
(650) 594-4242, www.limitededitionrs.com

Lion Brand Yarn Company
www.lionbrand.com

Liquitex® Artist Materials
(888) 4-ACRYLIC, www.liquitex.com

Little Black Dress Designs
(360) 894-8844, www.littleblackdressdesigns.com

Loersch Corporation USA
(610) 264-5641, www.loersch.com

Loew-Cornell, Inc.
(201) 836-7070, www.loew-cornell.com

LuminArte (formerly Angelwing Enterprises)
(866) 229-1544, www.luminarteinc.com

Ma Vinci's Reliquary
http://crafts.dm.net/mall/reliquary/

Magenta Rubber Stamps (wholesale only)
(800) 565-5254, www.magentastyle.com

Magic Scraps™
(972) 238-1838, www.magicscraps.com

Magnetic Poetry®
(800) 370-7697, www.magneticpoetry.com

Making Memories
(800) 286-5263, www.makingmemories.com

Manto Fev™
(402) 505-3752, www.mantofev.com

Marvy® Uchida/ Uchida of America, Corp.
(800) 541-5877, www.uchida.com

May Arts
www.mayarts.com

Maya Road, LLC
www.mayaroad.com

McGill, Inc.
(800) 982-9884, www.mcgillinc.com

me & my BiG ideas® (wholesale only)
(949) 883-2065, www.meandmybigideas.com

Michaels® Arts & Crafts
(800) 642-4235, www.michaels.com

Morning Star Stamp Company—no contact info

Mostly Animals Rubber Art Stamps
(209) 848-2542, www.mostlyanimals.com

Mrs. Grossman's Paper Company (wholesale only)
(800) 429-4549, www.mrsgrossmans.com

Mustard Moon™
(408) 299-8542, www.mustardmoon.com

My Sentiments Exactly
(719) 260-6001, www.sentiments.com

Nielsen & Bainbridge
(800) 927-8227, www.nielsen-bainbridge.com

Northwoods Rubber Stamps
(651) 430-0816, www.northwoodsrubberstamps.com

Nunn Design
(360) 379-3557, www.nunndesign.com

Office Depot
www.officedepot.com

Office Max
www.officemax.com

Offray
www.offray.com

Outdoors and More—no contact info

Outlines™ Rubber Stamp Company, Inc.
(860) 228-3686, www.outlinesrubberstamp.com

Paper Co., The/ANW Crestwood
(800) 525-3196, www.anwcrestwood.com

Paper House Productions®
(800) 255-7316, www.paperhouseproductions.com

Paper Loft
(801) 446-7249, www.paperloft.com

Pebbles Inc.
(801) 224-1857, www.pebblesinc.com

Penny Black Rubber Stamps, Inc.
(510) 849-1883, www.pennyblackinc.com

Pipe Dreamink
www.pipedreamink.com

Plaid Enterprises, Inc.
(800) 842-4197, www.plaidonline.com

Polyform Products Co.
(847) 427-0020, www.sculpey.com

Postmodern Design
(405) 321-3176, www.stampdiva.com

Prickley Pear Rubber Stamps
www.prickleypear.com

Provo Craft® (wholesale only)
(888) 577-3545, www.provocraft.com

Prym-Dritz Corporation
www.dritz.com

PSX Design™
(800) 782-6748, www.psxdesign.com

QuicKutz
(801) 765-1144, www.quickutz.com

Ranger Industries, Inc.
(800) 244-2211, www.rangerink.com

River City Rubber Works
(877) 735-2276, www.rivercityrubberworks.com

Royal® & Langnickel/Royal Brush Mfg.
(219) 660-4170, www.royalbrush.com

Rubba Dub Dub Embellishments & Art Stamps
(209) 763-2766, www.artsanctum.com

Rubber Stampede
(800) 423-4135, www.deltacrafts.com

Rubber Stamps of America
(800) 553-5031, www.stampusa.com

Rubberstamp Ave.
(541) 665-9981, www.rubberstampave.com

Rusty Pickle
(801) 272-2280, www.rustypickle.com

Sakura Hobby Craft
(310) 212-7878, www.sakuracraft.com

Sandylion Sticker Designs
(800) 387-4215, www.sandylion.com

Sanford® Corp.
(800) 323-0749, www.sanfordcorp.com

Savvy Stamps
(866) 44-SAVVY, www.savvystamps.com

Scenic Route Paper Co.
(801) 785-0761, www.scenicroutepaper.com

Scrap Ease®
(800) 272-3874, www.whatsnewltd.com

Scrap in a Snap™
(513) 829-6610, www.scrapinasnap.com

Scrappy Cat™, LLC
(440) 234-4850, www.scrappycatcreations.com

Scrapworks, LLC
(801) 363-1010, www.scrapworks.com

Scrapyard 329
(775) 829-1118, www.scrapyard329.com

SEI, Inc.
(800) 333-3279, www.shopsei.com

Serendipity Stamps, Inc.
(816) 532-0740, www.serendipitystamps.com

Silver Bow Creations—no contact info

Sonburn, Inc.
(800) 527-7505, www.sonburn.com

Speedball® Art Products Company
(800) 898-7224, www.speedballart.com

Staedtler®, Inc.
(800) 927-7723, www.staedtler.us

Stamp Accents—no contact info

Stamp A Mania Manufacturing
(505) 524-7099, www.stampamania.com

Stampa Rosa—no longer in business

Stamp Barn, The
(800) 246-1142, www.stampbarn.com

Stamp Craft—see Plaid Enterprises

Stamp Doctor, The
(208) 286-7644, www.stampdoctor.com

Stamp In The Hand Co., A
(310) 884-9700, www.astampinthehand.com

Stamp It!—no contact info

Stampabilities®
(800) 888-0321, www.stampabilities.com

Stampendous!®
(800) 869-0474, www.stampendous.com

Stampers Anonymous
(888) 326-0012, www.stampersanonymous.com

Stampin' Up!®
(800) 782-6787, www.stampinup.com

Stampington & Company
(877) STAMPER, www.stampington.com

Stamps by Judith
www.stampsbyjudith.com

Stamps Happen, Inc.®
(714) 879-9894, www.stampshappen.com

Stars & Stamps Forever
(858) 758-1488, starssstampsforever@yahoo.com

Stewart Superior Corporation
(800) 558-2875, www.stewartsuperior.com

Sticker Studio™
(208) 322-2465, www.stickerstudio.com

Stockwell—no contact info

Strathmore Papers
(800) 628-8816, www.strathmore.com

Sugarloaf Products, Inc.
(770) 484-0722, www.sugarloafproducts.com

Sunday International
(800) 401-8644, www.sundayint.com

Sweetwater
(800) 359-3094
www.sweetwaterscrapbook.com

Target
www.target.com

Therm O Web, Inc.
(800) 323-0799, www.thermoweb.com

Tidy Crafts
(208) 523-2565, www.tidycrafts.com

Timeless Touches™/Dove Valley Productions, LLC
(623) 362-8285, www.timelesstouches.net

Tsukineko®, Inc.
(800) 769-6633, www.tsukineko.com

USArtQuest, Inc.
(517) 522-6225, www.usartquest.com

Victorian Paper Company/Victorian Trading Co.
www.victoriantrading.com

Wal-Mart Stores, Inc.
(800) WALMART, www.walmart.com

Walnut Hollow® Farm, Inc.
(800) 950-5101, www.walnuthollow.com

Westrim® Crafts
(800) 727-2727, www.westrimcrafts.com

WFR Ribbon Corporation—no contact info

Winsor & Newton™
www.winsornewton.com

Wordsworth
(719) 282-3495, www.wordsworthstamps.com

Wübie Prints
(888) 256-0107, www.wubieprints.com

Xyron
(800) 793-3523, www.xyron.com

Index of Tips